W9-CFI-570

VINCENT'S
COOKBOOK

VINCENT GUERITHAULT
with JOHN MARIANI

TEN SPEED PRESS
BERKELEY, CALIFORNIA

*À ma mère, Anne Marie, et à mon père, Daniel, pour avoir été les premiers
à cuisiner pour moi. Et à Gilles, mon oncle, pour m'avoir encouragé.*

*I would like to offer special thanks to the following people who helped make this book
possible, either directly or indirectly: Jean & Doris Banchet, Wolfgang Puck,
Jacques Pépin, Penny Pfaelzer, and John Mariani; Charles Owen for always being
a willing taster; Bettie Stewart, Pearl Wallace, Donna Brannum, and Elaine Mills
for testing each recipe; Alexis Brunner and George Young at Ten Speed Press; and
my wife, Leevon, and my sons, Daniel and Nicolas.*

Copyright © 1994 by Vincent Guerithault

All rights reserved. No part of this book may be reproduced in any form
without the written permission of the publisher, except in the case of
brief quotations embodied in critical articles or reviews.

TEN SPEED PRESS
P. O. Box 7123
Berkeley, CA 94707

*Illustrations on pages 32, 33, 52, 53, 67, 87, 113,
121, 223, 225, and 240 are by Sara Manus.
Except for the illustrations listed above, illustrations throughout the book
are by the nineteenth-century woodcut artist Joseph Crawhill.*

*Design by Christine Taylor
Composition by Wilsted & Taylor Publishing Services*

LIBRARY OF CONGRESS CATALOGING-IN-PUBLICATION DATA
Guerithault, Vincent.
 Vincent's cookbook / by Vincent Guerithault.
  p. cm.
 Includes index.
 ISBN 0-89815-566-5
  1. Cookery, American—Southwestern style.   I. Title.
 TX715.2.S69G84   1994
 641.5979—dc20   94-8090
                                                               CIP

FIRST PRINTING 1994

1 2 3 4 5 6—99 98 97 96 95 94

Contents

Foreword

It may seem odd that the preeminent interpreter of modern Southwest cuisine is a classically trained Frenchman with a difficult last name who pronounces the word *chile* as "she-lay." But then, until a few years ago, Vincent Guerithault couldn't tell a *jalapeño* from a *habañero*. Yet, in the past five years, he has earned a formidable reputation as one of the most dynamic and inventive chefs in the Southwest. His restaurant, Vincent Guerithault on Camelback, in Phoenix, Arizona, is widely considered one of the best restaurants of any kind in the country.

At his first restaurant (which he did not own) in Pinnacle Peak, Arizona, he garnered national attention in the early 1980s when the food editor of the *New York Times,* Craig Claiborne, dined there and afterward wrote, "If one may judge a restaurant on the basis of one visit but in the company of five other guests, each of whom ordered a variety of dishes, I would declare Vincent's to be exceptional."

In those days, Vincent's food was nothing like what he cooks today. Indeed, when I first dined at his restaurant in 1982, I was surprised that this young, very shy chef was turning out such extraordinarily sophisticated haute cuisine in an elegantly decorated dining room forty-five minutes' drive into the desert outside Phoenix.

At the time there was little on Vincent's menu that would indicate his later style. His cooking was principally derived from the butter-and-cream-rich cuisine of his mentor, Jean Banchet of Le Français, outside Chicago, then one of the most highly regarded French restaurants in America. After he moved to Phoenix, Vincent began to see the possibilities, became familiar with the cornucopia of southwestern ingredients, and settled into a life in Arizona that included a beautiful American wife named Leevon who shook Vincent free of his formalistic culinary straitjacket.

As a chef trained in the exacting and rigid formalism of French kitchens, Vincent had to overcome certain prejudices and traditions before he could forge a new kind of cooking that took into consideration modern concepts of entertaining, taste, and nutrition. As he became more comfortable using exotic ingredients such as *chile* peppers, corn, cilantro, *masa,* and *jícama,* he was able to produce a hybrid cuisine based on the most exacting French techniques while loosening up those strictures that had once bound him to an exclusively classic kitchen. He presented plates with color and design, and the casual chic of his dining room attracted a sophisticated, well-traveled clientele who knew good food and fine wines.

During that period, many American chefs hopped on the southwestern bandwagon that had begun to gather some speed, but none possessed the training or the discipline of Vincent, who was able to apply a lifetime of French technique and craft to each ingredient, recipe, and presentation. Slowly he introduced southwestern elements into his cuisine, not as experiments at the customers' expense but as a natural evolution of his own taste and background. You will not find a dish on Vincent's menu or in this book that in any way seems contrived or unrefined. These are dishes he has perfected—indeed, several have become signatures that his customers won't let him remove from his menu. Each recipe has been thought through for a depth of taste, not for the kinds of razzle-dazzle special effects that are concocted merely to astound people and get the attention of the media.

By careful thought and constant attention to detail, Vincent has been creating an entirely new cuisine. Southwestern cookery had for some time been developing along the lines of a marriage between Californian novelties and traditional concepts of Mexican food, but it was Vincent who focused his cooking to absorb the flavors of the Southwest into a refined, sublimated cuisine that no one else in America had really attempted before. He took traditional standards such as the *tamale,* the *burrito,* and the *quesadilla* and made them over in his own style. He began to realize the affinities between *chiles* and European seasonings and the delectable textures to be achieved by adding ingredients such as shredded tortillas and *jícama* to his food.

His menus are sophisticated but unpretentious, innovative without ever lapsing into eccentricity. And for his restaurant he has compiled a wine list that has been judged one of the finest in the country, the wines matched impeccably to the kind of food he serves.

With all this, Vincent Guerithault has not been one to keep to his kitchen or hold his culinary "secrets" to himself. He is known among peers as one of the most generous, hardworking chefs in America and loves nothing better than to serve as an educator and to demonstrate his singular techniques and seasonings at such events as dinners at the James Beard Foundation House and the "De Gustibus" series of cooking classes held at Macy's in New York and San Francisco. For three years he served on the Food Board of the New England Culinary Institute as a consultant on the culinary and service curriculum.

Most recently Vincent has embarked upon a new venture—an authentic, French-style market next to his restaurant. Every Saturday morning from October to May the open-air market has stalls with vendors selling wine, organic produce, exotic lettuces, edible flowers, croissants, breads, pastries, and offerings from the restaurant.

Having achieved all this, Vincent felt it appropriate to write his own cookbook, and I was honored to be asked to participate. As someone who dines out most nights of the week and visits at least twenty American cities each year, I have become more and more convinced of Vincent's talents and vision. In working on this book with Vincent and Leevon, I have also become convinced that this is food that people can make at home with great success—food that fits perfectly into our modern way of life in which casual dining, bold flavors, grilled meat and fish, and a healthy regard for good ingredients are favored. The results, as this book shows, are wondrous—bursting with flavor and color, geared to the season, and presented with the flair that the Southwest is known for.

JOHN MARIANI

Southwestern Cuisine

Despite the certain simplistic reactions most people have when you mention "southwestern food," it is actually one of the more complex cuisines in the United States with deep roots in the region's historically diverse culture. Although many of the early influences on the region were based on Mexican traditions, even earlier cultures had developed a wide-ranging cookery based on the natural ingredients of the land.

The Native Americans who migrated into the Southwest twenty-five thousand years ago respected the land with a religious fervor that was tied to an anthropomorphic view that the animals of the region were both a gift of the gods and friends to man. Bison—incorrectly called *búfalo* (buffalo) by the Spaniards—antelope, deer, and rabbit, together with numerous species of birds, gave the Native Americans a rich and varied diet and an entire mythology. They built rituals and harvest festivals around the region's flora, especially corn, the life-supporting grain they called "Sacred Mother" and used in myriad ways over the entire length and breadth of the Americas. Corn reached the territory that is now the United States more than two thousand years ago, and the Zuñis believed it had miraculous powers: They would dust their doorways with cornmeal in the belief that it would repel the conquistadors. The Hopis cultivated at least twenty different types of corn, some to be ground into meal or flour, others to be eaten as porridge or roasted over a fire.

Just as essential to an understanding of Native American food culture is the *chile* pepper (*Capsicum annuum*), of which there are more than three hundred varieties. The word *chile* (preferred to *chili,* which refers to the Tex-Mex stew of meat and *chile* peppers) comes from the Nahuatl, *chilli.* Christopher Columbus found the natives of the New World cultivating the plant and using the fruit as a principal seasoning for their food, as they had been at least as early as 3300 B.C. It was reported in 1529 by a Spanish missionary that the Aztecs put *chile* peppers in everything they ate, including chocolate.

Oddly enough *chiles* may not have arrived in what is now the United States until they were brought in from Mexico by General Juan de Oñate, who founded Santa Fe in 1598. Whenever they arrived, they were immediately popular and are now ubiquitous throughout the Southwest. The Spanish, who reached Arizona in the mid-sixteenth century, brought their own food culture to the region. Most notably, a Jesuit priest, Father Kino, introduced cattle and sheep to Tucson about 1700. The Spanish fell in love with New World spices and hoarded them for their own use or for shipment back to Europe.

After Mexico ceded the territory to the United States in 1850 and the Apache raids against settlers ceased in 1886, settlers from the east brought their own European-derived cookery to Arizona, which became a state in 1912. Today the region's cuisine is extremely varied, from the popular steak and potatoes to the *chile*-pepper-laced, Mexican-influenced grub of the *cantinas,* the modern counterparts of the basic sa-loon and lunch room of the Old West.

After World War II Phoenix developed from a stiflingly in-temperate desert town to a fully air-conditioned resort city, and with affluence came the kinds of European restaurants that always follow new money. These were mostly of the "continental" stripe, posh dining rooms with uninspired menus full of *tournedos* Rossini, *quiche Lorraine,* and chocolate mousse. There were western-theme restaurants where everything on the menu had contrived cowboy names like "wrangler steak" and "chuck wagon T-bone." At one famous tourist trap the waiters were instructed to cut off the necktie of any man fool enough to wear one. There was a smattering of Italian places, Greek *tavernas,* Chinese eateries, and lots of Mexican spots (actually more Tex-Mex) where the only concession to Sonoran cookery was to serve combo platters with green, rather than red, *chile* sauce.

Things began to change for the better in the late 1970s when chefs across the Southwest started to use the regional products and ingredients that were to be found in profusion from Texas to California. Some, Mark Miller of Santa Fe's Coyote Cafe, for instance, paid local farmers to raise varieties of herbs and *chiles* that had long ago died out in the region; others, among them Dean Fearing of the Mansion on Turtle Creek in Dallas, Robert Del Grande of Café Annie in Hous-ton, Donna Nordin of Café Terra Cotta in Tucson, Jimmy Schmidt of the Rattlesnake Club in Denver, and Vincent Guerithault, were experimenting with a wondrous array of new dishes derived from traditional ones such as chicken-fried steak, guacamole, chili, sweet potato pie, *quesadillas,* barbecued beef, and *huevos rancheros.*

The public not only responded favorably to the novelty of these foods but also soon came to expect them of the restaurants in the region, so that, today in cities such as Phoenix, San Antonio, Denver, Aspen, and Albuquerque, almost every restaurant that is not geared to a European ethnic cuisine invariably serves some form of the New Southwestern Cuisine. It is no longer unusual to find *fajitas* stuffed with lobster or *enchiladas* with crab. Desserts, once heavy and too often fried in batter or served in *taco* shells, took on the refinement of French pastry, even if made with southwestern flavors, cinnamon, Mexican vanilla, and cornmeal in the crusts.

There is no substitute for a flavor that comes from an herb or vegetable that is fresh and indigenous to the Southwest, where the best beef and lamb in the world are raised, but fortunately it is easy enough for any American cook to come by most of the typically southwestern ingredients in the average supermarket; some of the exotica can be easily ordered by mail. A glossary, beginning on page 269, provides descriptions of regional ingredients that are used in the recipes. The typical techniques of barbecuing, sautéing, frying, and baking will be familiar to anyone who cooks with any degree of seriousness.

JOHN MARIANI

Introduction

When people eat at Vincent on Camelback they often wonder why a French-born chef came to Arizona to do southwestern cooking so far from his home in northeastern France. If someone had predicted twenty years ago that I would one day be in America working in a city I had then never heard of, I would have thought him absurd. Certainly, nothing in my childhood prepared me to cook *chimichangas* and *burritos*. When I was sixteen years old, I started my career in the south of France in the village of Les Baux-de-Provence. I did not really enjoy school and my parents were ready to let me try something new because they were tired of fighting with me about continuing my education. Through the help of a free-spirited uncle who loved good restaurants and fine dining, I got a job as an apprentice at Oustau de Baumanière, which was then rated with three stars in the Michelin guide. I considered myself very lucky and thought I would be in for a glamorous time. Was I ever surprised when I received my first paycheck—six dollars for a month's work! I was provided with room and board, which consisted of one small bedroom

with a cold-water sink and a communal bathroom for the five chefs I lived with.

The head chef was very difficult to work for, and we were constantly dodging flying pots and pans when something did not go right. I started out in the kitchen peeling potatoes and carrots and scrubbing the floors at night. Later I was promoted to dishwasher. The first cooking job I had was for the customers' dogs. In France it's acceptable to take a dog into a restaurant on a leash and to let it sleep under the table. The restaurant usually offers a plate for the dog, charging about five dollars.

That was my first experience at cooking. I was there for two months before I was permitted to work in the kitchen along with the other chefs, preparing "people" food. It was a grueling schedule—usually sixteen to eighteen hours a day, seven days a week. But there is no doubt that the training I received there and the demanding hours that I worked prepared me to be where I am today. I can do every job in my kitchen, so if anyone, from the dishwasher to the pastry maker, doesn't show up for work, I pitch in and do what has to be done.

After spending a year at Oustau, I went to Paris and worked at the famous Maxim's for two-and-a-half years. There I quickly learned that all the glamour is on the other side of the kitchen door. I worked hard and learned to do high-volume cooking, a skill that is crucial to a chef. I was then drafted into the French navy, where I served for a year as head chef aboard a ship. Even there the French penchant for good food is intact; the French sailors eat much better than those of any other country. After all, they have some of the best young cooks in France making their meals!

When my military service was completed, I returned to

Paris and went to work at Fauchon, the renowned gourmet shop and restaurant on the Place de la Madeleine, which carries more than twenty thousand food products. I also worked at several small restaurants in Paris where I learned how the individual proprietors and chefs can make such an extraordinary difference. It was while working at a small place on Ile Saint-Louis that I met Jean Banchet, who had established one of the most famous French restaurants in the United States—Le Français in Wheeling, Illinois. Jean was rebuilding Le Français, which had been destroyed by fire, and was looking for French-trained chefs to come and work for him. He invited me to go to Chicago and work for about six months. I thought it would be a great opportunity to see the United States and, as it would only be for six months, I could return to Paris as a "man of the world" and continue my career there.

Of course, I had no idea what life in America would be like and certainly knew nothing about running a business, either in France or America. There is no doubt that I would not be owning my own restaurant today were it not for Jean and his wife, Doris. Jean refined my culinary training and taught me about life in America, what Americans expected in restaurants, and how they differ from the French. It was an eye-opening experience. People tend to view dining differently in the two countries, although the food in Chicago is certainly a lot closer to what Europeans like than was the food then being served in Phoenix.

I stayed in Chicago with Jean for four years as his sous-chef, but I grew tired of the snow and the cold and was ready for a new adventure. A good friend of mine from France lived as a foreign-exchange student with a family who wintered in

Arizona. One day the family mentioned to my friend that they knew a person who was looking for a French chef to open a restaurant in Pinnacle Peak, Arizona. Knowing that I was weary of Chicago's windy winters, my friend called to see if I would be interested.

I had no idea where even Phoenix, Arizona, was, much less Pinnacle Peak. All I had heard about it was that it got very, very hot. I decided it couldn't be any hotter than the winters in Chicago were cold, so I applied for the job. I was very excited about being the head chef in a restaurant. But the owner had the strange notion of having me prepare French food in what was otherwise a Mexican restaurant, so that he would be able to offer both French and Mexican food. I knew nothing whatsoever about Mexican food. I had no idea what *tamales* and *enchiladas* were. In fact, I couldn't even pronounce the name of the restaurant, Oaxaca. But that didn't seem to matter: I had been hired to do the French food. It was hard to explain to my family back in France what I was doing, and they were sure that this was the end of my cooking career in America.

The concept of having French and Mexican chefs in the same kitchen just didn't work. Mexican food is much faster to prepare, and the cooks I worked with were not as concerned about the presentation of the food on the plates as we French are. There I was, trying to create dishes such as lobster with morels and lambs with truffles next to a chef who was rolling *burritos* and frying *tacos*—with mariachi singers serenading us in the background! It was a complete disaster when a party of four ordered dinner and three wanted Mexican food and one wanted French. The orders were never ready at the same time, and believe me, it was difficult to find a wine that went well with both *foie gras* and *tamales*. Eventually the owner of the restaurant agreed to separate the two cuisines. The Mexican restaurant stayed upstairs and the French moved downstairs and was named Vincent's French Cuisine. I was able to prepare my classic French dishes without distraction, and my food was very well received.

Before I knew it five years had passed. In the back of my mind I always knew that someday I would own my own restaurant. By late 1984 I had gained something of a national reputation, so I thought it was time to take the leap and spent the next year making plans. I found premises much closer to Phoenix and halfway to Scottsdale. With the location fixed, I had to decide on the kind of food I wanted to serve. I knew it was going to be something *very* different, something that could not then be found in Phoenix. As much as I'd complained about having to work with the Mexican chefs in Pinnacle Peak, I was fascinated by the food they were preparing because it was so new to me and I did enjoy the tastes. That is where my interest in southwestern cooking began.

In 1986, southwestern cuisine had not yet surfaced in Phoenix. Arizona was a perfect proving ground, because so many of the ingredients are indigenous to the area. I started experimenting with different spices and ingredients such as cactus, *jícama,* corn *masa,* and *chile* peppers, and used the ingredients in some of my French dishes and developed what we now called "French/Southwestern cuisine."

In January 1986, we opened for business. At first the menus reflected more of my French background, but as the years have passed, our menu has become more southwestern as we have become more familiar with the local spices and *chiles* and know how they can influence and enhance certain foods. We are, however, not fanatically southwestern, and try to keep our dishes subtle, so that any one ingredient or flavor is not overwhelming.

It was also in 1986 that I met Leevon Owen, the woman who would become my wife. At that time, Leevon was the executive administrator for a real estate firm and called me to cater for one of her company parties. Leevon was born and raised in Arizona and has greatly influenced what we are doing at Vincent's by helping me with my adaptation to southwestern tastes and inclinations. Leevon also gives me inspiration for some of my recipes. It was her idea to add *jalapeños* to an orange tart and that dish has been popular ever since. Leevon has had a hand in the interior design of our restaurant and much of the warmth and ambience is the result of her influence.

A few years ago, we noticed that many of our customers were asking that we serve their food with the sauce to the side or even with no sauce at all. So we developed what we call a "heart smart menu," which now accounts for approximately 20 percent of our dinner sales. (Recipes from that menu are marked with a ♥ in this book.) I have also tried to develop dishes for those people who, for medical reasons or by choice, are restricted to low-sodium, low-cholesterol food but want a change from the ubiquitous—and dull—grilled fish with lemon juice.

In writing this book, I've compiled recipes for some of my most popular dishes. They have all been carefully adapted to home cooking and have been home tested.

I sincerely hope you enjoy the flavors and textures and that you get a sense of the wonder that is the American Southwest (with a little French influence, of course!).

HORS D'OEUVRES

Among the most exciting foods in the world are hors d'oeuvres. And well they should be: They are designed to stimulate the appetite. At Vincent's we find that people are so delighted by the spicy, rich flavors of our hors d'oeuvres that they eat too many of them and end up losing their appetite for a big meal. I would suggest that you make sure that you'll have enough for seconds, thirds, even fourths when you make any of these recipes for a crowd.

CURRIED CHICKEN

IN BLUE CORN CUPS

*Many of the spices in curry powder, such as chiles, coriander,
and cardamom, are used frequently in Southwest cooking
so there is a natural East-West affinity in them. The blue corn
cup is not so far removed from those pliable, flat Indian breads.
This is real finger food and perfect for a summer's party.*

Corn Cups
6 tablespoons unsalted butter, at room temperature
4 ounces cream cheese, at room temperature
1 cup flour
½ cup blue cornmeal
Pinch of salt

Curried Chicken
3 whole, boneless chicken breasts, about 7 ounces each
3 tablespoons mayonnaise
1 tablespoon sour cream
2 tablespoons Bell Pepper Salsa (page 35)
1 tablespoon curry powder
24 cilantro leaves, for garnish

To prepare the corn cups, preheat the oven to 350°F.

Mix the softened butter and cream cheese. Combine the
flour, cornmeal, and salt and gradually add the dry ingredients to the cream cheese mixture. Knead the dough for approximately 2 minutes and then allow it to rest for 15 minutes.

Divide the dough into 24 pieces and roll each piece into a
1-inch ball. Press each ball into a 2-inch muffin mold to form
a cup. Make sure that the dough is as even as possible and

comes up the sides of the tins to the top. Bake the cups for approximately 15 minutes. Set aside to cool.

To prepare the filling, preheat the oven to 400°F.

Roast the chicken breasts for approximately 15 minutes, or until they are cooked through. Allow them to cool, remove the skin, and chop the meat finely.

Combine the chicken with the mayonnaise, sour cream, salsa, and curry powder. Spoon the chicken curry into the corn cups and garnish each cup with a cilantro leaf.

Makes 24 hors d'oeuvre servings

CACTUS & CORN SALSA ♥

Salsas are at the very heart of Southwest cooking, and they are used in more ways than any other condiment in the world. They may be simply served as a dip for tortilla chips, as a condiment with meat, poultry, fish or vegetables, or as a principal sauce in a main course. The tart-sweet flavors of salsas are common to Southwest versions and more often than not there is a hot pepper quotient that perks everything up.

*At Vincent's we use dozens of different salsas and never merely
depend on one or two basic varieties. The secret to good salsas is that
they are made with fresh ingredients. Even if left to marinate overnight,
it is essential that the finest seasonal ingredients be used.
Otherwise the individual tastes will not emerge from the salsa
and the whole thing becomes little more than a one-note mess,
as is the case with most bottled or canned salsas.
This cactus and corn salsa includes nopales, the paddles or "leaves"
of a prickly cactus. They can be purchased canned or bottled, though
it's always better to use them fresh. In some Mexican markets fresh
nopales are sold already cleaned. The recipe for grilled nopales on
page 187 includes directions for removing the prickles.*

1 cup steamed fresh or frozen corn kernels
1 cup cooked, chopped *nopales* (cactus paddles) (page 187)
1 teaspoon chopped cilantro
1 teaspoon peeled, seeded, and diced tomatoes
1 teaspoon chopped shallot
1 teaspoon chopped red bell pepper
1 teaspoon chopped yellow bell pepper
1 teaspoon chopped green bell pepper
1 teaspoon lemon juice
Salt and pepper

Combine the corn, *nopales,* cilantro, tomato, shallot, bell
peppers, and lemon juice. Add salt and pepper to taste. This
salsa is also good with goat cheese *nachos* (page 12).

Makes 2 1/4 cups

11

HORS D'OEUVRES

GOAT CHEESE NACHOS

Nachos *are among the world's most underappreciated foods.*
They may be a Tex-Mex staple and ballpark favorite, but they can
be made to taste as good as any French hors d'oeuvre you've ever had.
Goat cheese nachos *have been on our menu since we opened the restaurant.*
They're a great start because they whet the appetite
but aren't too filling. We put a very thin slice of jalapeño *pepper*
on top of each chip so that the peppers enhance rather than
overpower the taste of the cheese. These are delicious served with red and
green bell pepper sauces (page 55), avocado corn salsa (page 65),
or tomatillo *and corn salsa (page 129).*

3 ounces goat cheese
1 ounce cream cheese
1 tablespoon sour cream
1 tablespoon chopped parsley
1 tablespoon chopped *jalapeño* pepper
Salt and pepper
Fried corn tortilla chips (2 whole corn tortillas)

*P*reheat the oven to 275°F. Mix together cheeses, sour
cream, parsley, and *jalapeño*. Season with salt and pepper to
taste. Put a small spoonful of the mixture on each chip and
bake them in the oven for 5 minutes or until the cheese melts.

Serves 4

AVOCADO & CORN QUICHE

*Quiche is a specialty of the area in France where I was born and,
contrary to what they say, real men do eat quiche, especially
when they are as delicious and full-bodied as this one is.*

Pastry Dough
1 cup flour
1 teaspoon salt
½ cup butter
1 egg

Quiche Filling
1 cup fresh corn kernels or 1 cup thawed frozen corn
1 avocado, halved, pitted, peeled, and diced
1 tablespoon chopped cilantro
2 extra-large eggs ✍ 1 cup half-and-half
Salt and pepper ✍ Nutmeg

To make the pastry, mix the flour and salt together and rub in the butter by hand or using a food processor. Add the egg and let the dough rest for approximately 2 hours in the refrigerator.

Preheat the oven to 400°F. Roll out the dough on a floured board to ⅛-inch thickness and fit it into an 8-inch quiche pan. Prick the dough with a fork. Bake the shell for between 18 and 20 minutes, or until it is golden brown. Set the shell aside to cool and turn the oven down to 300°F.

To make the filling, cook the corn for 20 minutes in boiling water and drain thoroughly. Arrange the diced avocado, the corn, and the cilantro in the center of the quiche crust. Whisk the eggs until they are frothy, stir in the half-and-half, and season with salt and pepper to taste. Pour the egg mixture into the quiche shell over the avocado and corn. Sprinkle some nutmeg on top.

Bake the quiche for 25 minutes, until the mixture has set or a knife inserted comes out clean. Serve hot.

Serves 6

SKEWERS OF LAMB *with* ANCHO BUTTER

An ancho chile *is a dried* poblano. *Dried, the* chile *is a
very wrinkled dark brown, and when reconstituted, brick red.
The* ancho *has a mild, sweet flavor that is a little woody.
This butter made with pure* ancho chile *powder adds a remarkable
flavor to grilled lamb cooked on skewers over an open fire.*

4 bamboo skewers, soaked in water
1 tablespoon pure *ancho chile* powder
8 tablespoons (1 stick) butter, softened
1 teaspoon lemon juice
1 tablespoon chopped parsley
Salt and pepper
1 pound lamb loin, cut into 16 cubes
1 medium red onion, peeled and cut into sixteenths
1 medium red bell pepper, cut into 16 cubes
1 tablespoon olive oil

To make the *ancho* butter, combine the *chile* powder, butter, lemon juice, and parsley and add salt and pepper to taste. Form the mixture into a log, wrap it in plastic wrap, and store it in the freezer. The butter can be stored for several weeks.

On the skewers alternate the lamb cubes with pieces of onion and bell pepper; each skewer should have 4 cubes of each. Brush the skewers with olive oil and add salt and pepper to taste. Grill the skewers over a hot fire for a total of 5 or 6 minutes, turning them every couple of minutes. Set them aside for 2 minutes.

Serve each skewer with 2 slices of the *ancho* butter on top.

Serves 4

GRILLED SHRIMP *with*

CHIPOTLE MAYONNAISE

This is a simple dish but the combination of flavors is particularly good. The velvety chipotle *mayonnaise gives a smoky, sweet taste to the shrimp.*

8 bamboo skewers, soaked in water
32 small to medium-sized shrimp, peeled and deveined
1 tablespoon olive oil
Salt and pepper
½ recipe Chipotle Mayonnaise (page 63)
1 tablespoon chopped parsley

After preparing the shrimp (leave the heads on if you like), thread 4 shrimp on each skewer approximately 1 inch apart, making sure that the shrimp stay flat. Brush the shrimp with olive oil and add salt and pepper to taste. Grill the shrimp over a hot fire for approximately 1 minute on each side. Serve 8 shrimp per person with *chipotle* mayonnaise and chopped parsley on top.

Serves 4

SUN-DRIED TOMATO ROUNDS ♥

When unexpected guests arrive, this versatile spread is handy to have around.
With its snappy flavor, it kick starts the appetite when spread on
toast or country bread. You may even want to dip corn chips into it.

1 baguette
Olive oil
2 jars (6 ounces) sun-dried tomatoes
2 cloves garlic, minced
2 tablespoons grated Parmesan cheese
Fresh basil

Cut the baguette into ¼-inch-thick slices. Brush 1 side with olive oil, and broil until the bread is golden and crisp.

Purée the sun-dried tomatoes with their oil in a food processor or blender. Add the minced garlic and season to taste with freshly grated Parmesan cheese. Spread the purée on the baguette slices and garnish with fresh basil.

Serves 4

FIRST COURSES

Soups

Too often soups are the forgotten stepchildren on restaurant menus. At Vincent's we are very proud of our wonderful soups, which are made fresh every day and which contain a myriad of ingredients and flavors that perk up the appetite. Indeed, I think soup may be either the perfect appetizer or, when something light is desirable, the ideal main course at lunch with a salad and some good crusty bread.

CREAM OF AVOCADO SOUP

This soup is served chilled. The addition of a few pieces of diced tomato on top provides a touch of contrasting color.

2 large avocados, peeled and pitted
1 tablespoon olive oil
1 tablespoon chopped shallot
2 cups chicken stock (page 264), chilled
1 cup heavy cream
Salt, pepper, and freshly grated nutmeg
1 tomato, peeled, seeded, and diced, for garnish

Purée the avocados in a blender until smooth. In the olive oil, sauté the chopped shallot for between 2 and 3 minutes, but do not brown it. Set the shallot aside to cool.

In a large bowl, combine the avocado purée with the chilled chicken stock, cream, and sautéed shallot. Whisk until the mixture is smooth. Add the salt, pepper, and fresh nutmeg to taste. When ready to serve, top each bowl with diced tomato. Serve chilled.

Serves 4

CHILLED CUCUMBER SOUP *with*

SMOKED SALMON & FRESH DILL ♥

Because the flavor of the smoked salmon is rich, I've found that this soup works as well as a first course in winter as it does a main course in summer. Yet the soup is quite low in fat in spite of the luxurious appearance that is always impressive.

2 cups chicken stock (page 264)
1 tablespoon chopped celery
1 tablespoon chopped onion
½ teaspoon minced garlic
6 medium cucumbers, peeled and seeded
1 cup low-fat (2%) milk
2 tablespoons plain low-fat yogurt
2 tablespoons chopped fresh dill
¼ teaspoon salt
⅛ teaspoon white pepper
2 ounces smoked salmon
4 sprigs dill, for garnish

Simmer the chicken stock with the celery, onion, and garlic over medium heat for 20 minutes. Turn the heat down to low, add the cucumbers, and cook for an additional 5 minutes. Remove the mixture from the heat and purée it in a food processor or blender. Strain the purée through a fine sieve and chill it over ice. When the mixture is completely cool, whisk in the milk, yogurt, chopped dill, and salt and pepper. Keep the soup refrigerated.

To serve, garnish the soup with sliced smoked salmon and sprigs of fresh dill.

Serves 4

BLACK BEAN SOUP *with* GOAT CHEESE

This is a very hearty soup and is quite satisfying.
It should not be followed by a heavy meal. The younger goat cheeses
work well in this recipe because they melt right into the soup.
At the restaurant we sometimes combine this black bean soup with the
jalapeño cheese soup that follows because the contrasting colors of the
two soups look so good. When both soups are made, and they need to be
of the same consistency, pour them, using two ladles, simultaneously
into soup bowls, one color on each side. Serve hot.

1 pound black beans
1 quart chicken stock (page 264)
1 medium yellow onion, peeled and diced
1 carrot, peeled
1 whole bay leaf
1 *serrano chile* (peeled and seeded if less spiciness is desired)
1 cup heavy cream
Salt and pepper
6 ounces mild California goat cheese, cut into 6 slices, for garnish

Wash the beans and soak them overnight in water.

The following day, put the soaked beans into a large stock
pot with 1 quart water, the chicken stock, onion, carrot, bay
leaf, and *serrano chile*. Bring the mixture to a boil, then simmer
it for approximately 45 minutes. Remove the carrot and bay
leaf. Purée the remaining ingredients in a blender on low until the consistency is smooth. Add the cream and bring the
mixture to a boil. Add salt and pepper to taste. Serve hot with
a slice of goat cheese on top.

Serves 6

Jalapeño Cheese Soup

Excellent served on its own, this soup makes a dramatic presentation when served with black bean soup (page 21).

2 tablespoons olive oil
1 red onion, peeled and diced
Half a white leek, diced
Half a stalk celery, diced
6 cloves garlic, peeled and diced
1 quart chicken stock (page 264)
2 tablespoons butter
2 tablespoons flour
1 tablespoon chicken glaze (page 265) or 1 bouillon cube
¾ cup shredded *jalapeño*-flavored Monterey Jack cheese
¼ cup shredded sharp Cheddar cheese
¼ cup heavy cream
Salt and pepper
1 tablespoon pure Chimayó *chile* powder or cayenne pepper

Heat the oil in a large sauté pan. Sauté the onion, leek, celery, and garlic for 5 minutes. Add the chicken stock; bring the mixture to a boil, and simmer it for 30 minutes.

Melt the butter, stir in the flour, and whisk the mixture into the soup. Add the chicken glaze and simmer for 10 minutes. Purée the soup in a blender on low until it is smooth and add the cheeses, cream, salt, pepper, and *chile* powder. Simmer the soup until the cheeses are melted.

Serves 6

RED & YELLOW BELL PEPPER SOUP

This is another favorite because of the two-color effect of the soup in the bowl.
The balance between the two gives this soup a nice, delicate flavor.

2 large red bell peppers, roasted
2 large yellow bell peppers, roasted
2 tablespoons chopped shallot
2 tablespoons olive oil
4 cups chicken stock (page 264)
2 cups heavy cream
Salt and pepper

Keeping the colors separate, peel the roasted peppers, remove the seeds, and dice the flesh. Using 2 pans, sauté 1 tablespoon chopped shallot in half the olive oil in each pan; add the diced pepper, the red to one pan, the yellow to the other, and sauté for 2 minutes. Add 2 cups of the chicken stock to each pan and cook over low heat for 10 minutes. Add a cup of cream to each pan and simmer the mixtures for approximately 5 minutes. Add salt and pepper to taste. Separately, purée the mixtures in a blender until smooth.

When both soups are made, pour them, using two ladles, simultaneously into soup bowls, one color on each side. Serve hot.

Serves 8

GRILLED CORN SOUP *with*

ANCHO CHILE CREAM

*We usually serve our grilled corn soup in the winter because it is
a cream-based soup and a little heavier than our warm-weather soups.
This version is very rich and smooth, and we swirl* ancho chile
*cream in the center just for a touch of spiciness.
The former president of France, Valéry Giscard d'Estaing,
had this soup at the restaurant and enjoyed it so much that
he wrote to ask if I could send him some* ancho chile *powder—
not an ingredient easily found back in Paris.*

4 large ears corn, husks removed, or 2½ cups frozen corn kernels
2 cloves garlic
½ cup diced carrot
½ cup diced onion
¼ cup diced celery
1 *jalapeño* pepper, finely diced, or ½ teaspoon cayenne pepper
1½ cups chicken stock (page 264)
1 cup heavy cream or half-and-half
Ancho Chile Cream (recipe follows)

Grill the ears of corn for 5 minutes over a hot flame. Cut the corn kernels off the ears and combine the cut corn with the garlic, carrot, onion, celery, *jalapeño* pepper, and chicken stock in a heavy pan and simmer for 30 minutes. (If a less spicy soup is desired, remove the skin and seeds of the *jalapeño* before using it.) Add the cream and boil the mixture for 5 minutes. Purée the soup in a blender for approximately 1 minute and serve it hot with *ancho chile* cream.

Serves 4

Ancho Chile Cream

1 *ancho chile* or 1 teaspoon paprika
¼ cup heavy cream
1 tablespoon sour cream

Simmer the *ancho chile* and heavy cream together for 5 minutes. Purée the mixture in a blender and strain out the seeds. Cool and add the sour cream. Swirl 1 tablespoon of *ancho chile* cream over each serving of soup.

Garlic Soup♥

If you believe all the medicinal claims that have been made for garlic, this soup is better than Mom's chicken soup—even my French mother's! It is rich in garlic but, because the garlic has been cooked, the flavor is mild and aromatic. When buying garlic, choose firm, plump bulbs and make sure that they are dry. Once they have been removed from the bulb, individual cloves will keep for between three and ten days. Fresh garlic should be stored in an open container in a cool, dark place away from other foods. It will keep this way for approximately eight weeks, but when you notice the cloves starting to shrivel, it's time to use a fresh bulb.

4 heads garlic, cloves separated and peeled
2 small onions, peeled and diced
½ cup olive oil
1 medium baking potato, peeled and diced
4 cups chicken stock (page 264)
¾ cup grated Parmesan cheese ❧ Salt and pepper
4 slices French bread, toasted
1 bunch sage, chopped, for garnish

Blanch the garlic in boiling water for 5 minutes. Remove the garlic and set it aside.

In a saucepan, sauté the onions in ¼ cup of the olive oil until they are lightly browned. Add the potato, chicken stock, and blanched garlic. Simmer the mixture for approximately 20 or 25 minutes over low heat. Pour the mixture into a blender, add the remaining ¼ cup of olive oil, ½ cup of the cheese, and salt and pepper to taste.

Put a slice of toast in the bottom of each of 4 soup bowls. Top with chopped sage and the remaining ¼ cup cheese. Pour very hot soup over the toast and serve immediately.

Serves 4

WATERCRESS SOUP

Most often we serve this refreshing summer soup chilled, although it is also very good served hot. Watercress is available year round. Make sure that the leaves are a uniform color and show no signs of yellowing or wilting. It will keep refrigerated for up to five days.

2 bunches watercress, washed and stems removed
2 cups chicken stock (page 264)
1 cup heavy cream
Salt and pepper

Put the watercress into a small stockpot. Add the chicken stock and cream and bring the mixture to a boil. Reduce the heat and cook for between 4 and 5 minutes, stirring frequently. Transfer the mixture to a blender and blend until the soup is smooth.

This soup may be served hot or chilled.

Serves 4

Salads

It's not difficult to understand why salads are so much a part of southwestern cooking. The hot climate and the extraordinary freshness of the greens and vegetables in the West make a perfect combination for good, light, cool tastes. Salads form a very small part of French cooking; in America they serve as almost every course, from appetizer to main dish, and even follow the entrée instead of a dessert.

You'll find that several of the following recipes make perfect main-course salads at any time of year, but particularly when the seasonal harvest provides the best, ripest papayas, avocados, and corn.

Curly Endive Salad *with* Warm Sherry Vinaigrette

The leaves of curly endive, called frisée *in France, are slightly bitter
and have a prickly texture. Do not, however, mistake it for chicory,
which is another relative of the endive family. The smaller heads will
have a more delicate flavor than those that are slightly larger.
In Europe curly endive is often served blanched.
Perhaps that is why I choose to serve it with a warm
sherry vinaigrette that wilts the leaves slightly.*

4 small heads curly endive
½ cup diced uncooked bacon
½ cup sliced white button mushrooms
2 tablespoons sherry vinegar
Salt and pepper

Wash the curly endive and discard any green leaves, using
only the inside white and yellow leaves.

Sauté the bacon and mushrooms together until the mushrooms are tender and the bacon is crisp. Using a slotted
spoon, remove the bacon and mushrooms and set them aside.
Add the sherry vinegar to the fat. Bring the mixture to a boil,
taste for seasoning, and add salt and pepper.

Arrange the curly endive on 4 plates. Top each serving
with bacon and mushrooms, then drizzle some of the warm
sherry vinaigrette on top.

Serves 4

Papaya, Avocado, &
Grapefruit Salad *with*
Honey & Lime Vinaigrette

*We are fortunate to have fresh, locally grown grapefruit available
in Phoenix, so when I make this salad I pick some fresh grapefruit
from my garden and use them. It's a very refreshing salad,
and I like the contrast of the tartness of the grapefruit with the
sweetness of the papaya and the creamy flavor of the avocado.*

2 whole avocados, halved, pitted, and peeled
1 whole papaya, peeled, seeded, and quartered
2 medium grapefruit, peeled and segmented
1 tomato, peeled, seeded, and diced
1 cup *frisée*
Honey and Lime Vinaigrette (recipe follows)

*P*repare the vinaigrette and set it aside.

To arrange the salad, cut the avocado halves into ten slices
and fan the slices down the center of the plate. Slice the
papaya quarters on the bias very thin and fan the slices out
next to the avocado. Place 5 grapefruit segments next to the
avocado.

Top the avocado with one-fourth of the diced tomato. Arrange *frisée* around the rim of the plate, drizzle the salad with
vinaigrette, and serve chilled.

Serves 4

Honey & Lime Vinaigrette

2 tablespoons honey
Juice of 2 limes (about 3 tablespoons)
4 tablespoons walnut or olive oil
1 tablespoon sherry vinegar

Combine the honey, lime juice, oil, and vinegar, mixing
well with a whisk.

Makes ⅔ cup

Salad of Asparagus & Roasted Sweet Peppers *with* Honey & Sherry Vinegar Dressing♥

This is a very colorful presentation and makes a nice starter for a light luncheon. When buying asparagus make sure that the tips on the stem are not wilted or shriveled. Cook the asparagus only until the stem wilts a little. Add the dressing just before serving, because the acid in the vinegar will turn the asparagus yellow if added too far in advance. The simple, light dressing may be used for almost any salad. We use fresh, Arizona-made honey. A secret to distributing dressing evenly on your salad is to put it in a spray bottle and spray it all over your salad just before serving. This method also reduces the calories being served because one uses less dressing.

20 spears of asparagus, peeled
Half a yellow bell pepper, roasted
Half a red bell pepper, roasted
2 tablespoons chopped basil, for garnish
2 tablespoons diced tomato, for garnish
Honey and Sherry Vinegar Dressing (recipe follows)

*B*lanch the asparagus in boiling water for about 5 minutes, cooking just until the stems are flexible, and let it cool.

Peel the roasted bell peppers, remove any seeds, and cut into julienne strips. Using one-fourth of the different peppers per serving, weave a "mat" out of strips of yellow and red bell pepper. Place spears of asparagus across the top. Just before serving, drizzle with the dressing and garnish with chopped basil and diced tomato.

Serves 4

HONEY & SHERRY VINEGAR DRESSING

2 teaspoons honey
2 teaspoons sherry vinegar
2 tablespoons olive oil
Salt and pepper

Combine the honey, vinegar, and oil, mixing well. Add salt and pepper to taste.

Makes ¼ cup

BLACK BEAN SALAD♥

*We use black beans a lot at Vincent's, and I like this salad made
with them. It's healthful and very satisfying. You can be inventive
with the ingredients, as black beans go with a variety of flavors.
The bell pepper salsa is delightfully colorful because we use at least
three colors of peppers. Use as many as you can find in your market.
The salsa has a fresh, crunchy texture and is also delicious served with
chips, goat cheese nachos (page 12), quesadillas (page 81),
or on top of seafood. It will keep for four or five days if refrigerated.*

2 cups cooked black beans
1 cup Bell Pepper Salsa (recipe follows)
½ cup cilantro leaves
½ cup diced tomato
½ cup olive oil ✍ ¼ cup lemon juice
Salt and pepper

Mix the beans, salsa, cilantro, tomato, olive oil, and lemon
juice. Season with salt and pepper. Let the salad sit for at least
2 hours before serving.

Serves 4

Bell Pepper Salsa

1 red bell pepper
1 green bell pepper
1 yellow bell pepper
1 medium tomato
1 yellow hot *chile*
4 green onions
2 garlic cloves, peeled
2 tablespoons chopped cilantro
1 teaspoon sherry vinegar
1 tablespoon walnut oil
Salt and pepper

Core and dice the peppers, tomato, *chile,* green onions, and garlic very fine and combine all the vegetables. Add the cilantro. Stir in the vinegar and oil and season with salt and pepper.

Makes 2 to 3 cups

Jícama & Bell Pepper Salad ♥

This is a very colorful salad.
I particularly like the sweet, nutty flavor
of the jícama *with the mild, sweet bell pepper.*

1 green bell pepper
1 red bell pepper
1 yellow bell pepper
1 large *jícama*
2 tablespoons chopped flat-leaf Italian parsley
½ cup olive oil
2 tablespoons balsamic vinegar
Salt and pepper

Roast, peel, and julienne the bell peppers. Peel and julienne the *jícama*. Mix the *jícama*, bell peppers, and parsley. Combine the olive oil and vinegar and add salt and pepper to taste. Stir the dressing into the vegetable mixture and divide the salad among 4 plates.

Serves 4

Tomato & Cilantro Salad

Like basil, cilantro has a particular affinity for tomatoes and,
also like basil, there is no substitute for it and it must be fresh.

4 cups miniature round or teardrop-shaped tomatoes, washed and cut in half
½ cup chopped cilantro leaves
¼ cup chopped walnuts
½ cup walnut oil
2 tablespoons lemon juice
Salt and pepper

Mix the tomatoes, cilantro, and walnuts. Stir in the oil and
lemon juice and season to taste. Refrigerate the salad for 15
minutes before dividing it among 4 plates to serve it.

Serves 4

WATERCRESS SALAD *with*
CITRUS VINAIGRETTE ♥

Citrus vinaigrette adds freshness and tartness to the peppery watercress leaves. Because we have fresh citrus abundantly available in Arizona, I thought this would be a great way to use some for a refreshing salad that can be served year round.

2 bunches watercress, washed and stems removed
¼ cup diced orange segments
¼ cup diced grapefruit segments
¼ cup diced tomato
¼ cup olive oil
1 tablespoon lemon juice
1 tablespoon orange juice
Salt and pepper

Mix the watercress, orange, grapefruit, and tomato. Divide the mixture among 4 plates.

Mix together the olive oil, citrus juices, and salt and pepper to make a dressing. This can be done ahead of time and the mixture kept in the refrigerator. When you are ready to serve, drizzle the salads with approximately 1¼ tablespoons dressing for each serving.

Serves 4

WILD RICE & CORN SALAD

*This idea came from the side dish of wild rice with fresh corn
that we serve at the restaurant. We decided to try a salad with similar
ingredients and this is the result. Its added attraction is
that it may be prepared ahead of time and keeps well.*

½ cup olive oil
2 tablespoons sherry vinegar
Salt and pepper
2 cups uncooked wild rice
2 cups fresh corn kernels (about 4 ears)
½ cup peeled, seeded, and diced tomato
¼ cup chopped basil

Combine the olive oil and vinegar, add salt and pepper to
taste, and refrigerate the dressing for 2 hours before serving.

Boil the rice for approximately 45 minutes and let it cool.
Cut the kernels off the cobs and blanch them in boiling water
for approximately 5 minutes. Allow the corn to cool. Combine the rice and corn, and add the tomato and basil. When
you are ready to serve the salad, add the dressing and toss the
ingredients gently.

Serves 4

Grilled Sea Scallop Salad

with Papaya Dressing

*The secret to this salad is to brush the scallops with the papaya purée
the night before, letting them marinate overnight. Also, be careful
not to overcook the scallops because they can easily become tough.
They are done when they change from a pale beige color to creamy pink.
If they are too white, it's a sign that they have been soaked in water—
a deceptive gimmick done to increase their weight. They should
have a sweet smell and a fresh, moist sheen. Use your scallops
immediately after purchasing them and certainly within a day or two.*

One-fourth of a fresh papaya, seeds removed
1 pound fresh medium sea scallops
3 to 4 cups assorted salad greens, including *mâche*,
red oak-leaf lettuce, *frisée,* and watercress
1 teaspoon olive oil
Salt and pepper
Papaya Dressing (recipe follows)

The night before, prepare the papaya purée and marinate the
scallops. Peel and chop the papaya roughly, place it in a
blender, and reduce it to a purée. Brush the scallops with
1 tablespoon of the purée (refrigerate the remaining tablespoon for the dressing) and marinate them in the refrigerator
overnight.

When you are ready to prepare the salad, wash and dry all
the greens and arrange them on salad plates. Prepare the
dressing but do not refrigerate it.

Just before serving, brush the sea scallops with the olive

oil, add salt and pepper to taste, and grill the scallops over hot mesquite or charcoal, or sauté them, for approximately 1 minute on each side; do not overcook them. Arrange the scallops around the greens, pour the dressing over the greens, and serve immediately.

Serves 3 to 4

PAPAYA DRESSING

2 tablespoons olive oil
2 teaspoons lemon juice
1 tablespoon papaya purée
1 tablespoon chopped fresh basil
1 tablespoon diced tomato
Salt and pepper

Combine the oil, lemon juice, papaya purée, basil, and tomato. Season to taste with salt and pepper. Do not refrigerate the dressing; use it at once, at room temperature.

Makes ⅓ cup

Goat Cheese Salad *with*

Basil & Sherry Vinegar Dressing

Warm goat cheese may have become a cliché of trendy cooking, but it still tastes good. Include some bitter greens in the salad mix; they will complement the cheese.

6 to 8 cups mixed greens ❧ 8 ounces goat cheese
1 teaspoon coarsely ground black pepper
Basil and Sherry Vinegar Dressing (recipe follows)

*P*repare the dressing first and chill it.

When you are ready to serve the salad, preheat the broiler. Wash and spin the greens dry. Shake the chilled dressing well, toss the greens in the dressing, and arrange them on 8 plates. Roll the cheese in the pepper until the outside is well coated. Cut the cheese into 8 slices and arrange them on a baking sheet. Heat the cheese under the broiler for approximately 1 minute. Place the slices of hot cheese on the top of the greens and serve the salad immediately.

Serves 8

Basil & Sherry Vinegar Dressing

¼ cup sherry vinegar ❧ ¾ cup olive oil
1 teaspoon honey ❧ 1 tablespoon finely chopped basil
1 teaspoon salt ❧ ½ teaspoon ground black pepper

Combine the vinegar, oil, and honey, mixing well. Stir in the basil, salt, and pepper and refrigerate the dressing until it is well chilled.

Makes 1 cup

Sirloin Steak & Anasazi Bean Salad

A substantial salad, this might also be served as a main course.
If Anasazi beans—dark red and white mottled beans long cultivated
in the Southwest—are not available, any other pink bean will do.

1 pound Anasazi beans or other pink beans ❧ 1 cup diced uncooked bacon

1 red or green bell pepper, cored and diced

1 medium red onion, diced and peeled

2 cups fresh, canned, or frozen corn kernels

1 sprig rosemary or 1 teaspoon dried rosemary

1 tablespoon minced garlic ❧ 2 quarts water

2 cups chicken stock (page 264)

1 pound trimmed sirloin, cut into 1-inch cubes

2 tablespoons olive oil ❧ Salt and pepper

Wash the beans and let them soak overnight. The following day, drain the beans and put them into a large stock pot.

Over medium heat, sauté the diced bacon, bell pepper, and onion until the bacon is cooked and the onion translucent. Add this mixture to the beans together with the corn, rosemary, garlic, water, and chicken stock. Bring the ingredients to a boil and turn the heat down to a simmer.

Sauté the cubed sirloin in 1 tablespoon of the olive oil until the pieces are browned on all sides, approximately 2 minutes. Add the sirloin to the beans and simmer the mixture, uncovered, for between 45 minutes and 1 hour, until the beans are tender and the meat is shredded. Strain off the liquid and discard the rosemary sprig. Chill the salad and, just before serving, toss it with remaining tablespoon of olive oil.

Serves 6 to 8

GRILLED SHRIMP SALAD *with*

FRIZZLED TORTILLAS

*This is one of my favorite salads. I like it because the assorted greens
with the bell peppers and basil make it exceptionally refreshing, and the
fresh ginger gives it a slight Pacific or oriental flavor and the frizzled
tortillas a crunchy, southwestern texture. I am always looking for
interesting ideas and, after tasting a salad that my friend,
Dean Fearing, the executive chef of the Mansion at Turtle Creek
in Dallas, made with corn tortilla strips in it, it occurred to me
that I could get some great results by running the tortillas through our
pasta machine. It works beautifully, and people always wonder how
we are able to slice the tortillas into such tiny strips. We serve this
salad with shrimp, but duck, scallops, or chicken will work equally
well and cilantro may be substituted for the basil.*

4 small, fresh 6-inch blue corn tortillas
2 small, fresh 6-inch yellow corn tortillas
½ cup olive oil
1 tablespoon red bell pepper, diced
1 tablespoon green bell pepper, diced
1 tablespoon yellow bell pepper, diced
1 tablespoon fresh ginger, julienned
2 tablespoons chopped fresh basil
2 tablespoons sherry vinegar
Salt and pepper
5 to 6 cups assorted greens
(lamb's lettuce, red oak-leaf lettuce, arugula, and watercress)
1 pound fresh shrimp, cleaned and deveined
(or the equivalent of 4 large shrimp per person)
1 tablespoon peeled, seeded, and diced tomato, for garnish

To prepare frizzled tortillas, cut each tortilla in half and run the halves through a pasta machine on the lowest (linguini) setting to make thin strips. If a pasta machine is not available, slice the tortillas by hand: Stack the tortillas, roll them up, and slice the roll thinly. Be sure that the tortillas are cool and slightly moist. The longer they are exposed to air, the more difficult they will be to work with. If blue corn tortillas are not available, use 4 yellow tortillas. Sauté the strips in olive oil until they are crisp. Drain them thoroughly and reserve the warm olive oil, using 2 tablespoons of it for cooking the shrimp and the remainder for the salad dressing.

In a large salad bowl combine the bell peppers, ginger, basil, vinegar, and the reserved, warm olive oil. Toss the ingredients and add salt and pepper to taste. Add the tortilla strips and the greens. Gently mix and arrange on 4 serving plates.

Brush the shrimp lightly with the remaining 2 tablespoons olive oil and grill them over a very hot fire for approximately 1 minute; be careful not to overcook them. Serve the shrimp hot over the mixed greens and tortillas, garnishing each salad with some of the diced tomato.

Serves 4

Grilled Chicken Pasta Salad *with* Bell Pepper Dressing

This salad is delicious served warm or cold. We use chipotle *pasta, which complements the chicken nicely because it has a little spiciness to it. The bell pepper vinaigrette which is served with it makes a very colorful presentation. For a variation you can make the same salad using lemon-dill pasta (page 100), and fish in place of the chicken strips.*

4 boneless, skinless chicken breasts, approximately 4 ounces each
Olive oil
Half a recipe Chipotle Pasta (page 96)
2 tablespoons salt
Bell Pepper Dressing (recipe follows)

Brush the chicken breasts on both sides with olive oil. Grill them over a medium-hot grill or broil them for approximately 7 minutes on each side and then slice them into thin strips. Prepare the dressing.

When you are ready to serve, cook the pasta in 4 quarts of boiling water seasoned with 2 tablespoons of salt for between 30 seconds and 1 minute or until *al dente*. Drain the pasta, mix it with the dressing, and serve it with strips of chicken on top.

Serves 4

BELL PEPPER DRESSING

2 tablespoons diced red bell pepper
2 tablespoons diced green bell pepper
2 tablespoons diced yellow bell pepper
2 tablespoons chopped basil
2 tablespoons olive oil
2 teaspoons sherry vinegar
Salt and pepper

Combine the diced bell pepper and basil. Stir in the olive oil and vinegar and season to taste with salt and pepper.

Light Dishes

I call the following recipes first courses, but I find that they are so popular that many people order two or three different ones and then move right on to dessert. In any case, they make ideal light lunch or dinner dishes, full of flavor and texture, and are very easy to make. In fact, this is where I really like to show off.

GRILLED AVOCADO *with* GOAT CHEESE

The idea for this dish came to me while dining at Jeremiah Tower's Stars Restaurant in San Francisco. Until I tasted his delicious grilled avocado, I really hadn't thought about serving an avocado hot. When I returned to Phoenix, I experimented a bit and this is the result. Contrary to a fairly widely held belief, grilling an avocado will not make it bitter.

1 green bell pepper
1 red bell pepper
1 yellow bell pepper
¼ cup plus 1 tablespoon olive oil
4 avocados, halved, pitted, and peeled
Salt and pepper
Bell Pepper Salsa (page 35)
8 ounces soft goat cheese, cut into 8 pieces
Cilantro sprigs, for garnish

*P*reheat the oven to 400°F and prepare a hot grill.

Julienne the bell peppers and sauté them in about ¼ cup olive oil over medium heat for about 10 minutes. Cut the avocados in half, remove the seed, and peel them. Rub the avocados with the remaining olive oil and season them with salt and pepper. Grill the avocados about 4 minutes, 2 minutes each side. Remove them from the grill and place them on a baking sheet. Fill the center of each avocado with bell pepper salsa and place a slice of goat cheese on top of the salsa. Place the avocados in the oven for approximately 5 minutes or until the cheese is softened. Divide the julienned bell peppers among 8 serving plates, place the avocados on top, and garnish with cilantro.

Serves 8

49

Avocado Napoleon

The dessert napoleon is a creation of French haute cuisine.
It seemed quite possible to make a savory version that mimics the
creaminess and sweetness of the original with yogurt and avocado.
It worked beautifully.

½ cup plain, low-fat yogurt
4 California avocados, peeled, pitted, and diced
1 medium tomato, peeled and diced
One-third of a red bell pepper, roasted, peeled, and diced
One-third of a yellow bell pepper, roasted, peeled, and diced
¼ cup chopped cilantro
4 teaspoons lime juice
Salt and pepper
4 sheets phyllo dough
2 teaspoons olive oil
4 teaspoons honey
4 teaspoons Chimayó *chile* powder or paprika
Cilantro leaves, for garnish

The day before, put the yogurt into a coffee filter and let it drain overnight in the refrigerator.

To prepare the filling, mix the diced avocado, two-thirds of the diced tomato, the bell peppers, chopped cilantro, lime juice, salt and pepper, and the drained yogurt.

Preheat the oven to 400°F. For each serving, brush 1 sheet of phyllo dough with olive oil and then fold it to make a double layer of dough. Cut the dough into 3 squares, each measuring 4 inches to a side. Drizzle some of the honey onto each square and sprinkle the phyllo lightly with Chimayó *chile* powder. Bake for between 6 and 8 minutes or until they are golden.

To assemble each serving, place 1 tablespoon of the avocado mixture in the center of a plate and then place 1 of the phyllo squares on top. Build the rest of the napoleon by alternating the phyllo and the avocado mixture in the same manner, using 3 squares of pastry. Sprinkle a little Chimayó *chile* powder on the plate to decorate it and add a few whole leaves of cilantro and the remaining diced tomato as garnish.

NOTE: This recipe is included with the permission of the California Avocado Commission, for which it was originally developed.

Serves 4

Avocado Soufflés

A few years ago I was hired by the California Avocado Commission
to develop some low-calorie but tasty recipes for avocados.
I learned that, although avocados are mostly fat, it is
monounsaturated fat—a form of "good fat" that may in fact lower
cholesterol levels in the blood. And because an avocado has only
300 calories, it makes a delectably light soufflé, perfect for lunch
with a nice salad and good rolls on the side. As with any soufflé,
it is better to bake these just before serving so that they don't collapse.

4 avocados
Juice of 1 small lime
4 teaspoons flour
1 whole *jalapeño* pepper, roasted (page 266), peeled, and diced
4 egg whites
4 teaspoons salt
Juice of half a lemon
2 teaspoons olive oil
4 small whole *jalapeño* peppers, for garnish
1 small tomato, diced, for garnish

$\mathcal{P}$reheat the oven to 375°F.

Cut the avocados in half, discard the pits, and scoop out the flesh with a spoon, leaving the skins intact. Select the 4 best-looking skins for shells for the soufflés and discard the rest. Finely dice the avocado flesh and mix it with the lime juice, 2 teaspoons of the flour, and the chopped *jalapeño*.

In a separate bowl whip the egg whites with the salt and lemon juice. Gently fold the egg white mixture into the avocado mixture. Brush the inside of each empty avocado shell with olive oil and coat with the remaining flour. Divide the mixture among the shells and bake the soufflés for between 8 and 10 minutes.

Serve immediately, having garnished the soufflés with the whole *jalapeño* peppers and sprinkled diced tomato around the plate for color.

NOTE: This recipe is included with the permission of the California Avocado Commission, for which it was originally developed.

Serves 4

Black Bean Terrine

with Goat Cheese &

Red & Green Pepper Sauces

*Black or turtle beans are small beans with shiny skins and for this recipe
should be soaked overnight and then cooked the day before being puréed
for the terrine. Their rich taste is complemented by the creamy goat
cheese and the black and white colors offer a lovely contrast.
We serve the terrine at room temperature,
but it's equally good served warm.*

2 pounds (4¾ cups) black beans
1 whole onion
1 whole carrot
1 whole *jalapeño* pepper
4 eggs
2 tablespoons chopped cilantro
Salt and pepper
1 tablespoon olive oil
8 ounces mild California goat cheese, formed into a log
Red and Green Pepper Sauces (recipe follows)

Wash the beans and pick them over to remove any stones.
Soak the beans overnight in cold water. Discard the soaking
water and cook the beans in 2 quarts fresh cold water with the
onion, carrot, and *jalapeño* for 1 hour over low heat. Drain
and discard the liquid from the beans, onion, carrot, and pepper. Purée the beans in a food processor or blender until they
are smooth. Mix in the eggs and cilantro and add salt and pepper to taste.

Preheat the oven to 250°F.

Brush the sides of a terrine or a bread-loaf pan with olive oil and line it with parchment paper. Pour in half of the bean purée, put the goat cheese in center, and cover with the rest of the purée. Bake the terrine in a *bain marie* (set the terrine into a larger baking pan into which you have poured enough hot water to come halfway up the sides of the terrine) for 1 hour. Let the terrine cool and refrigerate it overnight before slicing it. Serve the terrine cold, sliced and garnished with both sauces on top.

Serves 8

RED & GREEN PEPPER SAUCES

2 red bell peppers, cored and diced
2 green bell peppers, cored and diced
2 cups half-and-half
Salt and pepper

Keeping the colors separate, combine the peppers and 1 cup of the half-and-half in each of 2 saucepans. Season with salt and pepper and cook over low heat until the peppers are tender. Still keeping them separate, purée the two mixtures in a blender; strain and serve chilled.

Makes ¾ to 1 cup of each sauce

CHILES STUFFED
with WILD MUSHROOMS *with*
SHALLOT-BUTTER SAUCE

The poblano chile *comes in a variety of sizes and shapes but most commonly is triangular, being wider toward the top and smaller at the bottom. It is fairly mild in taste and, when roasted beforehand, has a nice, "woody" taste that is enhanced here by the flavor of the mushrooms. Any variety of mushroom works well—even truffles— but wild mushrooms such as* shiitakes *or the less-expensive oyster mushrooms give the most flavor. The red, green, and yellow bell peppers in this dish give it a crunchy texture and add color. This is a good appetizer for those who want to tantalize their tastebuds but not overpower them with spiciness.*

4 *poblano chiles,* roasted (page 266)
1 small red bell pepper, diced
1 small green bell pepper, diced
1 small yellow bell pepper, diced
3 tablespoons olive oil
1 pound fresh wild mushrooms, preferably *shiitake*
or oyster mushrooms, washed and diced
Salt and pepper
Shallot-Butter Sauce (recipe follows)

Roast the *chiles* and set them aside.

To make the stuffing, sauté the bell peppers in hot olive oil for approximately 5 minutes. Add the mushrooms and cook the mixture uncovered over low heat for approximately 15 minutes longer. Season with salt and pepper to taste.

With a sharp knife make a small opening in the side of each *poblano chile* and stuff it with some of the wild mushroom mixture. To serve, pour some of the heated sauce onto a plate and arrange the *chile* in the center.

Serves 4

SHALLOT-BUTTER SAUCE

2 shallots
1 cup dry white wine
½ cup white wine vinegar
1 pound unsalted butter, cut into ½-inch cubes and softened
Juice of half a lemon
Salt and pepper

Finely chop the shallots and combine them in a sauté pan with the wine and vinegar. Reduce the liquid over low heat until the pan is dry and only the shallots remain; this will take about 10 minutes. Whisk in the butter a few pieces at a time, the lemon juice, and the salt and pepper and bring the sauce to a quick boil. Set the sauce aside, keeping it warm.

Makes 2 cups

Ratatouille Terrine *with*
Bell Pepper Vinaigrette

*This terrine makes a very impressive presentation because the colors are
so beautiful. I love terrines and decided to do one with the vegetables
that are more frequently combined in* ratatouille, *a dish that is not
that unusual in France and has taken on a certain chic
in American restaurants, especially in the West.*

2 cups beef and chicken stock (page 267), prepared a day ahead;
to be used at room temperature

2 green bell peppers

2 red bell peppers

2 yellow bell peppers

2 eggplants, peeled and sliced thin

2 pounds zucchini, sliced thin but not peeled

1 ¼ cups olive oil

2 heads garlic ❧ 2 artichokes

Juice of half a lemon

1 medium red onion, peeled and sliced

1 pound tomatoes ❧ 5 shallots, peeled and diced

1 bunch thyme, leaves stripped off and stems discarded

Salt and pepper

Bell Pepper Vinaigrette (recipe follows)

℘repare the stock a day ahead and refrigerate it overnight,
but remove it from the refrigerator in time to allow it to reach
room temperature before using it in assembling the terrine.
If the stock is chilled, it will be too gelatinous and will not
spread evenly.

Roast the bell peppers, allow them to cool, peel them, and
remove and discard the seeds. Slice the peppers thinly, keeping each color separate, and set aside unrefrigerated.

Setting aside 1 teaspoon of the olive oil for the garlic, heat 1 cup of the oil and in it sauté the eggplant and zucchini until the vegetables are browned. Set them aside on paper towels to cool and drain. Reserve the cooking oil for the onion and set the pan aside.

Preheat the oven to 350°F. Pour the reserved teaspoon of olive oil over the heads of garlic, wrap them in aluminum foil, and bake them for between 15 and 20 minutes. When the garlic is tender, unwrap the heads and set them aside until they are cool enough to handle. Separate the heads into cloves, peel the cloves, and set them aside, at room temperature.

Cook the artichokes in a large pot of boiling water to which has been added 1 teaspoon of salt and the juice of half a lemon. When they are tender (depending on the size, this will take about 20 minutes), remove the artichokes from the pan, set them aside until they are cool enough to handle, discard the outer leaves and chokes, and slice the hearts thinly. Set aside with the other vegetables, also at room temperature.

Reheat the oil left over from cooking the eggplant and zucchini and in it sauté the onion until it is lightly browned. Drain off any excess oil and set the onion aside to cool.

Blanch the tomatoes in boiling water, plunge them into ice water to cool them, and then peel and quarter them. Remove the seeds and pulp and reserve. Set the tomato quarters aside. Heat up the remaining ¼ cup olive oil in a clean pan and in it sauté the chopped shallots and the tomato seeds and pulp gently until the mixture has thickened; this will take about 15 minutes. Let the mixture cool and season to taste.

To assemble the terrine, have ready a glass or ceramic terrine or bread-loaf pan that measures approximately 9 by 5 by 3 inches deep. Make sure that all the vegetables are cool and dry and that the stock is at room temperature. Place a layer of eggplant in the bottom of the terrine and cover it with 1 tablespoon of stock. Add a layer of green peppers and cover that with a tablespoon of stock. Continue to layer the vegetables, covering each with a tablespoon of stock, in the following order: yellow bell peppers, sliced artichokes, garlic cloves, tomato quarters, tomato and shallot mixture, red onions, zucchini, and red bell peppers. Repeat the procedure until the terrine is full and finish with a last tablespoon of stock. Cover the terrine with plastic wrap and refrigerate it overnight.

When you are ready to serve it, slice the terrine with an electric knife and serve it, chilled, with bell pepper vinaigrette.

Serves 10 to 12

BELL PEPPER VINAIGRETTE

2 red bell peppers, cored and diced
5 tablespoons olive oil
1 tablespoon sherry vinegar
Salt and pepper

Combine the peppers, oil, and vinegar in a blender; purée the mixture and strain the purée, discarding the solids. Season with salt and pepper, to taste. Keep the vinaigrette chilled until you are ready to serve it.

Makes 1 to 1 1/2 cups

60

Sea Scallops *with*

Potato Cakes &

Cilantro Beurre Blanc

A combination of sea scallops and potatoes might be unexpected but the result, in this recipe, makes a very good and delicious appetizer. We serve them with cilantro beurre blanc, *but if you prefer, they can be served with no sauce at all and are still delicious.*

2 medium baking potatoes, peeled and diced
2 tablespoons butter
3 tablespoons olive oil
Salt and pepper
2 tablespoons chopped cilantro or 1 teaspoon dried parsley
4 large sea scallops
Cilantro *Beurre Blanc* (page 268)

Boil the potatoes in salted water for approximately 30 minutes or until they are tender. Drain and mash them, mixing them with butter, 2 tablespoons of the olive oil, salt, pepper, and cilantro. Divide the mixture into 8 portions and pat each portion into a cake. Sauté the potato cakes in a nonstick pan for approximately 3 minutes on each side or until they are golden brown. Keep them warm.

Brush the scallops with the remaining tablespoon of olive oil and grill or sauté them for approximately 1 minute on each side. Serve 2 potato cakes and 1 sea scallop on each plate, with cilantro *beurre blanc* spooned alongside.

Serves 4

Shrimp & Corn Fritters *with* Chipotle Mayonnaise

It's hard to imagine anyone not enjoying these scrumptious fritters. The sweetness of the corn and the texture and taste of the shrimp make them ideal for a party, and the batter may be made well in advance. And, despite what they may say, most people love fried food. These fritters can be made small for appetizers or larger and served as a main dish. Mayonnaise made from scratch really tastes much better than the store-bought kind. Flavored mayonnaises are interesting for enhancing foods and are easily made. Dill mayonnaise, which works well with seafood, and chipotle *mayonnaise, which we use here and on our burgers, are just a couple of examples.*

3 eggs separated
1 ½ cups flour
1 teaspoon olive oil
½ cup cold water
½ cup milk
1 tablespoon finely diced red bell pepper
1 tablespoon finely diced yellow bell pepper
1 tablespoon finely diced green bell pepper
½ cup fresh or frozen corn kernels
1 tablespoon chopped fresh cilantro or 1 teaspoon dried parsley
12 medium-sized shrimp, cleaned and chopped
Salt, cayenne pepper, and paprika
Oil for frying
Chipotle Mayonnaise (recipe follows)

Whip the egg whites to stiff peaks and set aside. Place the yolks in a mixing bowl, add the flour, olive oil, water, and milk, and mix until smooth. Add the diced bell peppers, corn,

cilantro, and shrimp. Season the mixture with salt, cayenne, and paprika.

Heat the oil in a deep pan until it reaches a temperature of 350°F. While the oil is heating, fold the whipped egg whites into the fritter mixture. Using 2 tablespoons, spoon the fritter batter into the oil and cook the fritters for 3 to 5 minutes or until they are golden brown. Serve immediately with *chipotle* mayonnaise.

Serves 8

CHIPOTLE MAYONNAISE

2 *chipotle chiles* canned in adobo sauce
1 egg yolk
1 tablespoon sherry vinegar
1 tablespoon prepared mustard
Juice of half a lemon, to 1 ½ tablespoons
Salt
1 cup vegetable oil

Combine the *chiles,* egg yolk, vinegar, mustard, lemon juice, and salt in a food processor. While the processor is running, add the vegetable oil very slowly to form an emulsion. Taste for seasoning.

Makes 1 ½ cups

BLUE CRAB CAKES *with*
AVOCADO CORN SALSA

There's only one secret to making great crab cakes:
Use a lot of crab and very little filler. What you do add to the crab
should have some snap to it without overpowering the delicate
flavor of the crabmeat. I prefer blue crab for this dish, but if it
is unavailable, substitute either Dungeness or king crab.
These cakes can be made up as bite-sized canapés.
The accompanying salsa provides additional excitement.
This is my interpretation of the traditional southwestern guacamole.
The word guacamole *is a Mexican-Spanish adaptation of a*
Nahuatl word and means avocado sauce. We add the lemon to
keep the avocado from discoloring, but the salsa never stays
around long enough for that to happen.

1 pound blue crab meat, picked over for cartilage
1 tablespoon chopped shallot
1 tablespoon diced red bell pepper
1 tablespoon diced yellow bell pepper
1 tablespoon diced green bell pepper
¼ cup plus 1 tablespoon bread crumbs
2 extra-large eggs
1 teaspoon low-fat, plain yogurt
Salt and pepper
2 tablespoons olive oil
Avocado Corn Salsa (recipe follows)

Mix the crabmeat together with the shallot, bell peppers,
1 tablespoon of the bread crumbs, the eggs, and the yogurt.
Season to taste. Form the mixture into 8 cakes.

Using the remaining ¼ cup bread crumbs, dust each cake and sauté them for 3 minutes on each side over low heat in the olive oil. Serve the cakes hot with avocado corn salsa.

Serves 8

AVOCADO CORN SALSA

1 cup steamed fresh corn kernels
1 cup diced avocado
1 teaspoon chopped cilantro
1 teaspoon diced tomato
1 teaspoon chopped shallot
1 teaspoon chopped red bell pepper
1 teaspoon chopped yellow bell pepper
1 teaspoon chopped green bell pepper
1 teaspoon lemon juice
Salt and pepper

Combine the corn, avocado, cilantro, tomato, shallot, and bell peppers. Add lemon juice and salt and pepper to taste. Serve immediately.

Makes 2¼ to 2½ cups

LOBSTER CHIMICHANGAS

A chimichanga *is a burrito that has been deep fried, and it's reputed to have first been made at a restaurant in Tucson called El Charro in the 1950s. Like many preparations in Mexican cookery, the* chimichanga *(which in translation means, somewhat inelegantly, "toasted monkey") may be filled with any number of ingredients such as beef, chicken, or seafood. I thought it would be fun to do something a little more upscale with the* chimichanga *and came up with the idea of using lobster, which has proven to be immensely popular. The nice thing about this recipe is it can be made in miniature portions and is perfect for bite-sized appetizers or hors d'oeuvres at a cocktail party. They can easily be made in advance and frozen, cooked or uncooked, to be reheated in minutes or deep-fried just before serving. If you are cooking for a crowd, consider varying the fillings: chicken and shrimp may be used interchangeably with the lobster.*

¾ pound fresh lobster meat
1 large leek, white part diced
⅓ cup heavy cream
Salt and white pepper
4 flour tortillas, 7 inches in diameter
2 ounces goat cheese, cut into 4 portions
2 cups vegetable shortening
Cilantro *Beurre Blanc* (page 268)

*B*lanch the lobster meat for 2 minutes in boiling water and set it aside. Blanch the diced leek for 1 to 2 minutes to soften. Pour the cream into a heavy pan and cook it over medium-high heat for several minutes until it thickens. Add the blanched leek and season to taste. Allow the mixture to cool.

To assemble the dish, spread the center of each tortilla with a quarter of the reduced cream and leek mixture. Place a portion of the goat cheese and a quarter of the lobster meat slightly off-center on each tortilla. Fold 2 sides of the tortillas over the filling, roll them up tightly, and secure each roll with a toothpick.

Heat the shortening to about 365°F in a deep pot and deep-fry the *chimichangas* for 3 to 4 minutes, or until they are cooked through and a deep golden brown. Drain briefly on paper towels. Serve the *chimichangas* with cilantro *beurre blanc*.

Serves 4

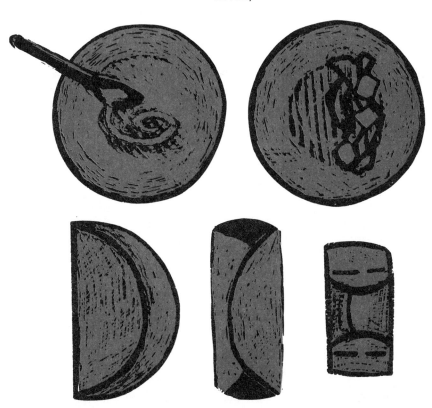

Tequila- & Lime-Cured Salmon *with* Citrus & Cilantro Vinaigrette

Asked to present some recipes using cactus and tequila for a meeting
of the American Institute of Wine and Food in New York,
I began experimenting with dishes using tequila, a spirit made
from the agave plant which grows around Tequila, Mexico.
I soon found that tequila makes a wonderful marinade for salmon
because of its high alcohol content. Gravlax is raw salmon that has
been "cooked" in a marinade, usually a salt mixture. Salmon left in
a tequila marinade for forty-eight hours will be cured and have a
delicious, slightly spicy flavor. Served with blue corn muffins,
it makes a delightful lunch dish or a starter at dinner. I serve this
vinaigrette because the citrus flavors taste great with the tequila.

1 whole salmon fillet, weighing between 12 and 14 ounces
4 tablespoons kosher salt ❧ 2 tablespoons sugar
1 teaspoon chopped garlic
1 tablespoon diced ginger
4 green onions, diced
2 whole *serrano chiles,* diced
6 sprigs fresh cilantro
½ cup tequila
Zest and juice of 3 medium limes
2 tablespoons sherry vinegar
Citrus and Cilantro Vinaigrette (recipe follows)
Blue Corn Muffins (page 203)

*P*lace the salmon fillet in a shallow pan and sprinkle the salt
and sugar over it. Top with the garlic, ginger, green onions,
chiles, and cilantro. Mix the tequila, lime juice and zest, and
vinegar and pour the mixture over the fish. Cover with plastic

wrap and place another pan on top to weight down and flatten the salmon. Refrigerate the salmon for 24 hours, turning the fish every 12 hours and being sure to replace the pan on top of the fish each time.

When the salmon is ready, it will be lighter in color. Slice it very thinly and arrange the slices on a plate. Top with citrus and cilantro vinaigrette and serve with blue corn muffins on the side.

Serves 6

CITRUS & CILANTRO VINAIGRETTE

Half a grapefruit
1 orange
1 lemon
1 lime
1 teaspoon honey
1 tablespoon sherry vinegar
3 tablespoons olive oil
1 tablespoon chopped cilantro
Salt and black pepper

Juice the grapefruit, orange, lemon, and lime and combine the juices in a mixing bowl. Add the honey, vinegar, olive oil, and cilantro and mix well. Adjust the seasoning with salt and black pepper. Refrigerate the vinaigrette until you are ready to serve.

Makes 1 1/4 cups

FOIE GRAS *with*

BLACK BEANS & GINGER

*A perfect example of what I call my style of southwestern French
cooking, this recipe combines the quintessential French luxury
ingredient—foie gras—with the humble southwestern black bean.
Foie gras is the fattened liver of a goose or duck and may be ordered
fresh from a wonderful company called D'Artagnan, Inc., in Jersey
City, New Jersey (the telephone number is 1-800-DARTAGNAN).
The foie gras comes from a producer in the Hudson Valley, New York.*

1 pound (2 ½ cups) black beans
8 cups chicken stock (page 264)
Salt and pepper ·
8 ounces *foie gras,* cut into 4 slices
1 tablespoon julienned fresh ginger
2 tablespoons sherry vinegar
1 tablespoon heavy cream
1 teaspoon chopped fresh parsley or ½ teaspoon dried parsley
1 tablespoon diced tomato, for garnish

Clean the beans and soak them overnight in water to cover. Drain the soaked beans and cook them in the stock over medium heat for approximately 1 hour, or until tender. Strain the mixture, reserving the stock, and purée the beans in a food processor or blender until the mixture is smooth. If the beans are too dry, add some of the reserved stock. Add salt and pepper to taste.

Sauté the *foie gras* in a very hot, dry pan for approximately 30 seconds per side. (There is no need to add oil to the pan; the *foie gras* has enough fat.) Set the *foie gras* aside, keeping it warm. In the same pan, using the fat yielded by the *foie gras,* fry the ginger until it is crisp. Set the ginger aside and use the same pan for making the sauce.

Pour the vinegar into the remaining *foie gras* fat. Add the cream and cook over medium heat until it has thickened. Taste for seasoning; you may want to add salt and pepper. Add the parsley.

To serve, divide the black beans evenly among 4 plates. For each serving, place 1 slice of *foie gras* on top of the beans, garnish with ginger and a small quantity of diced tomato, and pour some sauce around the *foie gras.*

Serves 4

Potato & Duck
Foie Gras Terrine

I have a special place in my cooking for foie gras *and always use the best I can find (page 70). The presentation of this dish is beautiful and it's worth the time it takes to prepare it.*

6 large baking potatoes
1 cup chopped shallots
2 tablespoons chopped green onions
1 tablespoon olive oil
Salt and pepper
1 pound fresh duck *foie gras*
Nutmeg
Mixed greens tossed with Honey and Sherry Vinegar Dressing (page 33)

$\mathcal{P}$eel and boil the potatoes. Purée 4 of the potatoes with a little of the cooking liquid while they are still hot and set them aside. Cut the remaining 2 potatoes into slices approximately ⅛ inch thick and set them aside. Sauté the shallots and green onions in hot olive oil until golden brown. Add salt and pepper to taste. Stir the shallot mixture into the puréed potatoes, taste, and adjust the seasoning if necessary. Set the mixture aside.

Wash the *foie gras* thoroughly and remove the veins from the inside. Season well with salt, pepper, and nutmeg. Line a 9 by 5 by 3-inch terrine (or a bread-loaf pan) with plastic wrap. Layer potato slices overlapped in a fan pattern over the bottom and up the sides of the pan. Coat the potato slices with a thin layer of potato purée. Fill the terrine with the *foie gras,* making sure that it is compact. Top with the remaining

potato purée. Cover the top of the terrine with plastic wrap, sealing it tightly against the ingredients. Refrigerate the terrine overnight.

The following day, when you are ready to serve, preheat the oven to 450°F and butter 6 pieces of parchment paper, each measuring about 6 inches square. Arrange the parchment on a baking tray and set aside.

Turn the terrine out onto a cutting board. Remove the plastic wrap and, with an electric or a serrated knife, slice the terrine into 6 equal slices. Place each slice on a piece of parchment paper. Bake the terrine for between 6 and 8 minutes, on one side only. Immediately turn the slices onto serving plates, remove the parchment paper, and serve the terrine hot, with the mixed greens.

Serves 6

CHICKEN PIZZAS *with*
PESTO, MOZZARELLA, BELL PEPPERS,
& SUN-DRIED TOMATOES

*Wolfgang Puck, the owner of the celebrated restaurants Spago in Los Angeles
and Postrio in San Francisco, made it possible for many chefs to treat the
once lowly pizza as a canvas for exciting ideas. By taking something
considered just a cut above fast food, Wolf made it into food for gourmets.
Thus was born the "designer pizza," and now you'll find them made with
almost any topping—not every one a good idea. At our outdoor market in the
restaurant's parking lot we even sell our pizzas by the slice, and the three
pizza recipes I've included here are among our most popular. They're quite
easy to make at home. This pizza gets its distinctive flavor from the
basil pesto that is spread liberally on top of the dough. I use the
sun-dried tomatoes because they add just a touch of sweetness.
We make our pizzas in eight-inch rounds, but you can make them
pretty much any size you wish for individual servings.*

2 boneless chicken breasts, 5 to 6 ounces each

2 teaspoons olive oil

Salt and pepper

Dough for four individual pizzas (page 78)

⅛ cup cornmeal

Half a red bell pepper, seeded and diced

Half a yellow bell pepper, seeded and diced

Half a green bell pepper, seeded and diced

½ cup basil pesto (page 94)

1 pound fresh mozzarella cheese, grated

2 ounces sun-dried tomatoes

2 bunches fresh basil leaves, chopped

$\mathcal{P}$reheat the oven to 450°F. Brush the chicken breasts with 1 teaspoon of the olive oil and season them with salt and pepper. Bake the chicken for approximately 10 minutes on each side.

While the chicken is cooking, roll out the balls of pizza dough on a lightly floured surface. The pizzas should be between 6 and 8 inches across. Sprinkle the cornmeal lightly on 2 baking sheets and place the pizza rounds on top. Set aside.

When the chicken is cooked, remove it from the oven and set it aside until it is cool enough to handle. Then remove the skin and bones and discard them. Chop the chicken meat coarsely.

Turn the oven up to 475°F.

Sauté the bell peppers in the remaining teaspoon of olive oil over medium heat for approximately 3 minutes. Place 2 tablespoons of basil pesto on each pizza round and spread it to cover. Layer with equal quantities of chicken, mozzarella cheese, bell peppers, and sun-dried tomatoes. Season the pizza with salt and pepper. Bake for between 10 and 12 minutes or until the crust is golden brown. When the pizzas are ready, sprinkle each with 1 tablespoon of the fresh basil and cut it into 8 slices.

Makes 4 individual pizzas

Duck Pizzas

Confit d'oie is the precursor to my recipe for duck confit.
Originally devised to use up the geese that were raised for foie gras,
of which there were far too many, even on one farm, to be eaten fresh,
the recipe yields a preserve that can be stored safely, without
refrigeration. Few people would consider roasting a duck especially,
for a pizza, which is, almost by definition, a quickly made snack food.
With a crock of confit at hand, even duck pizza is still a
quickly made snack in spite of the exotic topping.

⅛ cup yellow cornmeal
Dough for 4 individual pizzas (page 78)
1 pound mozzarella cheese, shredded
1 tomato, diced ❧ Half a red bell pepper, diced
Half a green bell pepper, diced
Half a yellow bell pepper, diced
¼ cup chopped fresh basil
2 cups shredded duck *confit* (page 142) ❧ ¼ cup olive oil

Preheat the oven to 400°F. Sprinkle a small quantity of cornmeal onto each of 2 baking sheets to prevent the dough from
sticking. Roll out the pizza dough to make 4 circles, each measuring between 6 and 8 inches across. Put the pizza rounds on
the baking sheets and layer equal quantities of the ingredients on them in the following order: cheese, tomato, bell peppers, fresh basil, and duck *confit*. Drizzle a small quantity of
olive oil over each pizza and bake them for approximately 15
minutes or until they are lightly browned. Cut each pizza into
8 wedges and serve immediately.

Makes 4 individual pizzas

VEGETABLE PIZZAS

These might have been called ratatouille *pizzas as the toppings are
made with the identical ingredients; only the cooking method differs.
Traditionally,* ratatouille *is a slowly cooked mélange of the vegetables.
For these small pizzas, the vegetables are sautéed quickly in under ten minutes.*

⅛ cup yellow cornmeal
Dough for 4 individual pizzas (page 78)
¼ cup olive oil ❧ 1 red onion, peeled and diced
1 red bell pepper, seeded and diced
1 yellow bell pepper, seeded and diced
1 large eggplant, diced ❧ 2 medium zucchini, diced
1 tomato, seeded and diced ❧ 4 cloves garlic, minced
2 tablespoons chopped basil ❧ 1 ⅓ cups grated mozzarella cheese

Preheat the oven to 400°F. Sprinkle the cornmeal on 2 baking sheets and set them aside. Roll out the pizza dough and
shape it into 4 rounds, measuring between 6 and 8 inches
across.

To make the topping, heat the olive oil over medium-high
heat in a large skillet. Sauté the onion until it is translucent.
Add the bell peppers and sauté them for approximately 3 or 4
minutes. Add the eggplant and zucchini and sauté for an additional 3 or 4 minutes. Add the tomato, garlic, and basil for
the last minute of cooking.

To assemble the pizzas, put ⅓ cup cheese on each round of
pizza dough. Cover with a quarter of the vegetable mixture.
Bake the pizzas for approximately 10 minutes or until the
crust is golden brown. Cut into slices and serve immediately.

Makes 4 individual pizzas

Basic Pizza Dough

In a pinch you can use a good-quality store-bought pizza dough,
but nothing tastes as good as a freshly made crust.
The dough may be frozen in individual batches for use at any time—
as can the entire pizza if you have the room in your freezer.

1 envelope (¼ ounce) active dry yeast
1 tablespoon sugar
1 ½ cups warm water
3 ¼ cups flour
½ teaspoon salt
¼ cup olive oil

*I*n a small bowl combine the yeast and sugar. Add the water and stir to mix. The yeast should be bubbling within 5 minutes; if it is not, discard the mixture and start again with a new envelope of yeast.

Put 3 level cups of the flour into a large bowl and add the salt. Make a well in the center of the flour; pour the yeast mixture into the well, and add the olive oil. Stir with a wooden spoon until all the flour is incorporated and the dough begins to hold. When the dough is still soft but holding together, turn it out onto a lightly floured work surface.

Begin to knead the dough gently, adding as much of the remaining ¼ cup flour as you need until the dough is no longer sticky. (The dough should be too soft rather than too stiff.) Continue kneading until the dough is smooth, shiny, and elastic.

Roll the dough into a ball and put it into a large, oiled bowl. Turn the dough once to coat it with oil. Cover with plastic wrap, put in a warm, draft-free place, and let rest until it has doubled in bulk (between 1 and 1½ hours). When the dough has doubled, punch it down and reshape into a ball. Cover and refrigerate until it has doubled in bulk again; this will take between 20 minutes and 1 hour.

When you are ready to make the pizzas, divide the dough into 7 equal-sized balls, weighing approximately 4 ounces each. Use one ball of dough for each individual-size pizza. Any dough not needed can be frozen in plastic wrap.

Makes 28 ounces dough; 7 individual pizzas

LOBSTER & WATERCRESS TACOS

*Until I came up with this delicious way of presenting a traditional
lobster and watercress salad, we didn't have any* tacos *on our menu.
I like watercress for its slightly bitter and peppery flavor with the richness
of the lobster meat. When buying watercress, make sure that the leaves
have a deep green color and show no signs of yellowing or wilting.
The lobster meat in this recipe can be replaced by strips of
grilled chicken breast, grilled shrimp, or duck* confit.

8 corn tortillas

Oil for frying

2 bunches fresh watercress, cleaned and stems removed

1 cup diced tomato

1 cup chopped basil

1 tablespoon diced yellow bell pepper

1 tablespoon olive oil

1 teaspoon lemon juice

8 ounces cooked, diced lobster meat

Salt and pepper

To make the shells for the *tacos,* fold the tortillas in half and
deep-fry them in hot oil until they are crisp. Make sure that
while the tortillas are being fried, the two halves do not stick
together; there should be enough space between the two
folded halves for the filling.

To make the filling, combine the watercress, tomato, basil,
and bell pepper. Stir in the oil and lemon juice and mix in the
lobster meat. Season to taste with salt and pepper. Fill the
prepared taco shells and serve at once.

Serves 4

SHRIMP QUESADILLAS

The quesadillas *we serve at* Vincent's *are my interpretation.*
Traditionally in Mexico quesadillas *are corn tortillas folded*
over a filling inside. As we serve them, they are open-faced flour
tortillas that have been slightly browned to give them
a crunchy texture like the thin pizza crust you'll find in Italy.

4 small, 6-inch flour tortillas
1 pound fresh shrimp (approximately 16 medium), cleaned and deveined
8 ounces mozzarella cheese, shredded
½ cup chopped fresh basil
½ cup diced tomato
½ cup olive oil
Salt and pepper

*P*reheat the oven to 300°F.

Sauté the tortillas in 1 tablespoon of the olive oil until both sides are browned. Remove the tortillas. Add about 3 table-spoons olive oil and sauté the shrimp for approximately 1 minute, stirring constantly. Drain the shrimp and slice each one in half lengthwise. Mix the cheese, basil, tomato, and shrimp. Top each tortilla with one-fourth of the mixture. Sprinkle the remaining olive oil evenly on the tortillas and heat them up in the oven for approximately 5 minutes, or until the cheese is melted. Slice and serve hot.

Serves 4

Chimayó Chicken Quesadillas
with Papaya & Cilantro Salsa

*Chimayó is a small town in New Mexico known for its chiles,
a variety of the long green New Mexico chile that has been
grown in the Chimayó village for so long that it has developed
distinctive characteristics found nowhere else. These quesadillas
are excellent when served hot with a chilled salsa.
When buying papayas look for those that are rich in color and
give slightly when pressed. Store them in the refrigerator and
use them as soon as possible. The salsa also works well with fish
(we serve it with our grilled 'ahi tuna) or chicken and even with pork.*

2 medium, 8-inch flour tortillas
2 tablespoons olive oil
1 boned, skinned breast of chicken, weighing approximately 6 ounces
2 teaspoons pure Chimayó *chile* powder   Anaheim
4 ounces mozzarella cheese, thinly sliced
2 tablespoons diced green bell pepper
2 tablespoons diced red bell pepper
2 tablespoons diced yellow bell pepper
Salt and pepper
Papaya and Cilantro Salsa (recipe follows)

*P*reheat the oven to 300°F.

Sauté the tortillas in 1 tablespoon of the olive oil until they
are golden brown on both sides. Add the rest of the olive oil
to the pan and sauté the chicken breast over medium-high
heat for 10 minutes. Sprinkle both sides with 1 teaspoon of
chile powder. When the chicken is cooked, let it cool slightly
and chop the meat into small chunks.

To prepare, layer the ingredients on the tortillas as follows: mozzarella cheese, chopped bell peppers, and shredded chicken breast. Season with the remaining teaspoon of *chile* powder, salt, and pepper.

Bake the *quesadillas* in the oven for 10 minutes. Cut each into 8 wedges and serve hot with papaya and cilantro salsa.

Serves 4

PAPAYA & CILANTRO SALSA

1 papaya
Half a red bell pepper
Half a yellow bell pepper
Half a green bell pepper
1 small tomato, peeled and seeded
2 bunches cilantro, chopped coarsely
1 tablespoon olive oil
Juice of 1 lime
Salt and freshly ground black pepper

Peel the papaya, cut it in half, and remove the seeds. Cut the papaya into ¼-inch dice and place in a bowl. Dice the bell peppers and tomato finely and add them to the papaya. Add the cilantro, olive oil, lime juice, salt, and pepper. Mix well and check the seasonings. Cover the salsa and refrigerate it until you are ready to serve it.

Makes 2 cups

Smoked Salmon Quesadillas

Simplicity itself, these quesadillas *are enlivened by the horseradish cream I developed to go with them. The combination of sour cream and goat cheese gives it a very smooth taste and texture. Adjust the amount of horseradish to your taste. The sauce also goes very well with beef dishes and makes a good sandwich spread.*

4 medium, 8-inch flour tortillas
2 tablespoons olive oil
Horseradish Cream (recipe follows)
4 large, thin slices smoked salmon
Chopped dill, for garnish

Sauté the tortillas in the olive oil for approximately 1 minute on each side to brown them slightly. Spread horseradish cream evenly over each tortilla. Arrange the smoked salmon over the horseradish cream and sprinkle with chopped dill. Cut each *quesadilla* in quarters and serve immediately, 2 quarters per person.

Serves 8

Horseradish Cream

2 ounces (⅓ cup) mild goat cheese
1 tablespoon grated fresh or purchased bottled horseradish
1 tablespoon sour cream
1 teaspoon chopped dill ❧ Salt and pepper

Mix the cheese, horseradish, sour cream, and dill. Add salt and pepper to taste.

Makes ½ cup

DUCK QUESADILLAS

A quesadilla should be a simple snack, even simpler than a pizza.
A couple of tablespoons each of three different colors of bell pepper would
be no trouble for a restaurant where peppers are used in various dishes.
To make this feasible at home, where you would probably not light up
the grill to roast a few pieces of bell pepper, consider another approach.
Roast several peppers at once, peel and seed them,
and then store them, separated by color, in the freezer.
They keep well and will be at hand, already prepared.

2 flour tortillas, 8 inches in diameter
2 tablespoons olive oil
⅔ cup grated mozzarella cheese
1 cup shredded duck *confit* (page 142)
2 tablespoons chopped, roasted green bell pepper
2 tablespoons chopped, roasted red bell pepper
2 tablespoons chopped, roasted yellow bell pepper
Salt and pepper

*P*reheat the oven to 300°F. Sauté the tortillas in 1 tablespoon
of the olive oil until they are golden brown on both sides.

Arrange half of the mozzarella cheese, the duck *confit,* and
the bell peppers on each of the tortillas. Season with salt and
pepper to taste.

Bake the *quesadillas* in the oven for 10 minutes, or until the
cheese is bubbly. Cut each *quesadilla* into 8 wedges and serve
hot.

Serves 4

RATATOUILLE TAMALES

On my first job in Phoenix, I worked alongside several
Mexican chefs and quickly learned about things like tamales.
One of the dishwashers used to make tamales *for himself late at night*
after the dinner service. They were the best I've ever tasted and became
my inspiration for this dish. A tamale *is any of a variety of meats, vegetables,*
or seafood wrapped in a dough of corn masa, *then steamed in a corn*
husk or banana leaf until the masa *is nice and moist but not gummy.*
I've seen tamales *served in just about every imaginable form, as a*
main course with meat or seafood and as a dessert with apple or other
fruit fillings. In Mexico the variety ranges from pumpkin to peanuts—
there is no limit. At Vincent's we use a good, commercially
prepared masa harina *of the kind you can easily find at a gourmet*
shop or fine market. We've also found it easier to roll our tamales
in parchment, as they steam nicely this way, are easy to store,
and parchment is more readily available than corn husks or banana
leaves. Then we use a corn husk for the presentation. But you must
warn those not familiar with tamales *or corn husks; I once served*
these in New York and a gentleman ate the entire corn husk and
then complained because he found it to be tough!

½ cup olive oil ∾ ¼ cup finely diced zucchini
¼ cup finely diced eggplant ∾ ¼ cup finely diced yellow bell pepper
¼ cup finely diced red bell pepper ∾ ¼ cup finely diced green bell pepper
¼ cup finely diced white onion ∾ ¼ cup peeled, seeded, and finely diced tomato
1 bay leaf ∾ 1 teaspoon chopped garlic
Salt and pepper ∾ 1 recipe *masa* dough (recipe follows)
8 dried corn husks or 8 sheets of parchment paper measuring 3 by 4 inches*
Cilantro *Beurre Blanc* (page 268)

*It is easier to use parchment paper for cooking and the corn husks as a garnish.

$\mathcal{H}$eat the olive oil in a skillet and sauté each of the vegetables separately for 3 minutes. Combine all the sautéed vegetables in a bowl and add the bay leaf and garlic. Season with salt and pepper to taste and let the mixture cool. While the filling is cooling, prepare the *masa* dough.

Spread *masa* dough about ⅛ inch thick over each corn husk or sheet of parchment paper and spread ⅛ of the *ratatouille* mixture over it. Roll up the husk or parchment and secure the ends by twisting them. Steam the *tamales* for 15 minutes and serve them hot with cilantro *beurre blanc*.

Serves 8

MASA DOUGH

2 cups *masa harina*
3 tablespoons sour cream
10 tablespoons (1 ¼ sticks) soft butter
1 teaspoon salt
1 teaspoon ground white pepper
1 teaspoon paprika
1 teaspoon cayenne pepper
1 cup chicken stock (page 264) or canned chicken broth

In a mixing bowl, combine the *masa harina,* sour cream, soft butter, salt, pepper, paprika, and cayenne. Slowly add the chicken stock until the *masa* is the consistency of a thick paste.

Makes 2 pounds dough, enough for 8 tamales

DUCK TAMALES *with* CILANTRO

BEURRE BLANC

Over the years I've had fun experimenting with different kinds of tamales. Our most popular are duck tamales filled with homemade duck confit (page 142). I add some raisins and Anaheim chiles to the confit to give it a little more personality. If you don't care for duck, the shredded meat from grilled chicken legs can be substituted. Senator Barry Goldwater comes to the restaurant often and he is so fond of our duck tamales that he once took a dozen with him on a trip to New York. Fortunately they freeze well.

1 recipe *masa* dough (page 88) ❧ 2 cups duck *confit* (page 142)
1 tablespoon chopped cilantro ❧ 1 tablespoon seedless raisins
1 tablespoon roasted, peeled, and chopped New Mexico (Anaheim) *chile* (page 266)
Salt and pepper
8 dried corn husks or 8 sheets of parchment paper measuring 3 by 4 inches*
Cilantro *Beurre Blanc* (page 268)

*P*repare the *masa* dough; set it aside while mixing filling.

Place the duck *confit* in a mixing bowl, and add the cilantro, raisins, and *chile*. Season with salt and pepper to taste.

Spread the *masa* dough about ⅛ inch thick on each corn husk or piece of parchment paper. Spread the duck filling about ¼ inch thick over the *masa*. Roll up the corn husk or parchment to enclose the dough and filling and twist the ends to secure them. Steam for approximately 15 minutes and serve with cilantro *beurre blanc*.

VARIATION
To make chicken *tamales,* substitute the shredded meat of 6 grilled chicken legs for the duck *confit*.

Serves 8

*It is easier to use parchment paper for cooking and the corn husks as a garnish.

SHRIMP TAMALES *with*
DILL BEURRE BLANC

In preparing these tamales, *be careful not to overcook the shrimp when making the filling. The* tamales *themselves will be steamed for fifteen minutes, ample time for the shrimp to finish cooking if they are left slightly underdone when sautéed.*

1 recipe *masa* dough (page 88)
1 pound headless shrimp, cleaned and diced
1 tablespoon olive oil
1 tablespoon chopped dill
Salt and pepper
8 dried corn husks or 8 sheets of parchment paper measuring 3 by 4 inches*
Dill *Beurre Blanc* (page 268)

*P*repare the *masa* dough and set it aside while cooking the shrimp.

Sauté the shrimp in hot olive oil for approximately 2 minutes on high. Add the dill and salt and pepper to taste. Remove from the heat.

Spread the *masa* about ⅛ inch thick on top of each corn husk or piece of parchment paper, spread the shrimp filling about ¼ inch thick on top and roll up the wrapping to enclose the filling, twisting the ends to secure them. Steam for approximately 15 minutes and serve with dill *beurre blanc.*

Serves 8

*It is easier to use parchment paper for cooking and the corn husks as a garnish.

Pasta

Over the past decade pasta has become such a staple of American menus that it is clearly no longer used only for Italian dishes. Pasta is marvelously adaptable to almost any sauce and the myriad shapes store-bought dry pasta comes in make it something you can have with meat, fish, or vegetables every day of the year.

The novelty at our restaurant is not that we make our own pasta fresh every day (something that is not hard to do at home if you have a simple pasta maker), but that we vary the flavors. We make one basic pasta dough at Vincent's and then flavor it with basil, *chipotle, chiles,* or lemon and dill, so that the flavors and colors are all very different.

BASIL PASTA

*In Europe my mother used basil a great deal and this pasta
reminds me of the wonderful pastas with basil pesto
that are so common from Genoa to Nice.*

2 cups flour
1 cup fresh basil leaves
4 extra-large eggs
1 tablespoon olive oil
¼ teaspoon salt

Mix the flour and fresh basil leaves in a food processor. Add
the eggs and mix. Slowly add the oil and salt. Process until the
mixture forms a small ball around the blade. It may be necessary to add 1 or 2 teaspoons water.

Put the dough on a lightly floured work surface and knead
it until it is silky and not sticky. It may be necessary to add a
little flour to keep the dough from sticking. Wrap the dough
in plastic wrap and allow it to sit for approximately 30 minutes before using. The dough can be refrigerated for up to 2
days or frozen.

To make pasta, divide the dough into 6 pieces so that it will be easier to work with. Roll each piece into a ball and put it through the widest setting of the pasta machine to flatten it. Put the flattened sheets of dough on a drying rack or a lightly floured cloth and allow them to dry for about 10 minutes before making noodles.

Set the pasta machine to the desired setting (the ¼-inch *fettuccine* size is recommended) and cut the dough into noodles. Let them dry on a drying rack until they are to be cooked. (Uncooked noodles can be kept in a dry place for several days before being used or they may be frozen.)

To cook, put the noodles into a large pot of boiling, salted water for approximately 3 minutes or until *al dente*.

Makes 1 ¼ pounds; 6 to 8 servings

BASIL PASTA *with* PESTO

*If you like basil, this is a blissful feast, requiring nothing
more than a glass of wine and some good bread.*

½ recipe Basil Pasta (page 92)
¼ cup pine nuts
1 pound fresh basil, washed thoroughly
1 head garlic, divided into individual cloves and peeled
½ cup olive oil

Make the pasta and set the noodles aside to dry while making the pesto.

Pour the pine nuts on a baking sheet and toast them under the broiler for 2 or 3 minutes, until they are golden brown. Shake the pan after the nuts have been cooking for about 1½ minutes so that they brown evenly.

Strip the basil leaves from the stems and place the leaves in a food processor or blender. Add the toasted pine nuts, the garlic cloves, and the oil. Purée the ingredients for about 2 minutes, until the mixture is smooth.

Cook the noodles in a large pot of boiling, salted water for approximately 3 minutes or until they are *al dente*. Drain, stir in the pesto, and serve at once.

Serves 4

Basil Pasta *with* Tomatoes, Garlic, Pine Nuts, & Cilantro

The unusual combination of basil and cilantro,
both pungent herbs on their own,
makes for a strong, well-flavored dish.

½ recipe Basil Pasta (page 92)
¼ cup olive oil
2 tablespoons chopped garlic
1 tablespoon pine nuts
1 medium tomato, blanched, peeled, and diced
¼ cup chopped cilantro
Salt and pepper

Make the pasta and set the noodles aside to dry while making the sauce.

In a frying pan, heat the olive oil and sauté the garlic over medium heat for 3 or 4 minutes. Add the pine nuts and cook for a minute. Add the tomato and continue cooking for 2 more minutes. Add the cilantro and salt and pepper to taste, stir quickly, and remove the pan from the heat.

Cook the noodles in a large pot of boiling, salted water for approximately 3 minutes or until they are *al dente*. Drain and toss lightly with the sauce. Serve hot.

Serves 4

CHIPOTLE PASTA

The chipotle *pasta has a beautiful burnt orange color
and the* chipotles *impart a rich, velvety taste, giving the pasta
a little spice that is still not overwhelming to the palate.
We usually serve it with veal or shrimp—foods that will not
compete with the rich flavor of the* chipotle.

2 cups flour
¼ cup *chipotle chiles* canned in adobo sauce
4 extra-large eggs
1 tablespoon olive oil
¼ teaspoon salt

Mix the flour and *chipotles* in a food processor. Add the eggs
and mix. Slowly add the oil and salt. Process until the mixture
forms a small ball around the blade. It may be necessary to
add 1 or 2 teaspoons water.

Put the dough on a lightly floured work surface and knead
until it is silky and not sticky. It may be necessary to add a little flour to keep the dough from sticking. Wrap the dough in
plastic wrap and allow it to sit for approximately 30 minutes
before using. The dough may be refrigerated for up to 2 days
or frozen.

To make the pasta, divide the dough into 6 pieces so that it
will be easier to work with. Roll each piece into a ball and put
it through the widest setting of a pasta machine to flatten it.
Put the flattened sheets of dough on a drying rack or a lightly
floured cloth and allow them to dry for about 10 minutes before making noodles.

Set the pasta machine to the desired setting (the ¼-inch
fettuccine size is recommended) and cut the dough into noo-

dles. Let them dry on a drying rack until they are to be cooked. Uncooked noodles can be kept in a dry place for several days before being used or they may be frozen.

To cook, put the noodles into a large pot of boiling, salted water for approximately 3 minutes or until *al dente*.

Makes 1 ¼ pounds pasta; 6 to 8 servings

CHIPOTLE PASTA *with*

BABY VEGETABLES & BEURRE BLANC

This dish can be made in installments:
the pasta made ahead, the vegetables prepared,
and even the reduction for the sauce made beforehand.

Half a recipe Chipotle Pasta (page 96)
¼ cup olive oil
16 baby carrots, peeled and blanched
16 baby turnips, peeled and blanched
16 asparagus spears, blanched
16 pea pods
16 baby zucchini
16 miniature teardrop-shaped tomatoes
Salt and pepper
Beurre Blanc (page 268)

Make the pasta and set the noodles aside to dry while preparing the vegetables.

Heat the olive oil in a large skillet and sauté the vegetables for 2 minutes. Add salt and pepper to taste.

Cook the noodles in a large pot of boiling, salted water for approximately 3 minutes or until they are *al dente*. Drain, stir in the sautéed vegetables and serve with *beurre blanc*.

Serves 4

Chipotle Pasta *with*

Grilled Shrimp

Shrimp and chile *peppers are perfect together.*
This same recipe, with the shrimp served with ancho chile
butter instead of the chipotle *pasta, appears as an hors d'oeuvre.*

Half a recipe Chipotle Pasta (page 96)
32 small to medium-sized shrimp, peeled and deveined
8 bamboo skewers, soaked in water
1 tablespoon olive oil
Salt and pepper
1 tablespoon chopped parsley

*P*repare the pasta and set the noodles aside to dry while grilling the shrimp.

After cleaning the shrimp (leave the heads on if you like), thread 4 shrimp on each skewer approximately 1 inch apart, making sure that the shrimp stay flat. Brush the shrimp with olive oil and add salt and pepper to taste. Grill the shrimp over a hot fire for approximately 1 minute on each side.

Cook the pasta in a large pot of boiling, salted water for approximately 3 minutes, or until *al dente*. Drain and serve with the shrimp, garnishing each serving with parsley.

Serves 4

Lemon-Dill Pasta

*This pasta has a zesty flavor that works well with fish and chicken.
It's also delicious chilled for salads or made into ravioli filled with mild goat cheese.*

2 cups flour ❧ ½ cup chopped fresh dill or 1 tablespoon dried dill
2 tablespoons grated lemon zest ❧ 4 extra-large eggs
1 tablespoon olive oil ❧ ¼ teaspoon salt

Mix the flour, dill, and lemon zest in a food processor. Add the eggs and mix. Slowly add the oil and salt. Process until the mixture forms a small ball around the blade. It may be necessary to add 1 or 2 teaspoons water.

Put the dough on a lightly floured work surface and knead until it is silky and not sticky. It may be necessary to add a little flour to keep the dough from sticking.

Wrap the dough in plastic wrap and allow it to rest for approximately 30 minutes before using. The dough can be refrigerated for up to 2 days or frozen.

To make pasta, divide the dough into 6 pieces. Roll each piece into a ball and put it through the widest setting of a pasta machine to flatten it. Put the flattened sheets of dough on a drying rack or a lightly floured cloth and allow them to dry for about 10 minutes before making noodles.

Set the pasta machine to the desired setting (the ¼-inch *fettuccine* size is recommended) and cut the dough into noodles. Let the noodles dry on a drying rack until you are ready to cook them. (Uncooked noodles can be kept in a dry place for several days before being used or frozen.)

Cook the noodles in a large pot of boiling, salted water for approximately 3 minutes, or until *al dente*.

Makes about 1¼ pounds pasta; 6 to 8 servings

Lemon-Dill Pasta *with*

Grilled Chicken Strips

*Unlike sauced dishes in which the pasta is merely there
to hold up the sauce, this dish depends on a well-flavored pasta.
The chicken is almost a garnish.*

Half a recipe Lemon-Dill Pasta (page 100)
4 boneless chicken breasts, each weighing about 6 ounces, skin on
1 tablespoon olive oil
Salt and pepper
1 tablespoon chopped dill

*P*repare the pasta and set the noodles aside to dry while grilling the chicken.

Brush each chicken breast with olive oil and add salt and pepper to taste. Grill the chicken over a hot fire for a total of between 10 and 12 minutes, turning the breasts after approximately 5 or 6 minutes. Set the chicken breasts aside for a few minutes and then remove the skin. Slice each into about 5 thin strips.

Cook the noodles in a large pot of boiling, salted water for about 3 minutes, or until *al dente*. Drain and serve topped with the strips of chicken and garnished with chopped dill.

Serves 4

Lamb Ravioli *with* Goat Cheese & Basil & Pine Nut Sauce

This dish combines a lot of international flavors and traditions.
Lamb with goat cheese is part of the Greek culinary culture,
ravioli are Italian, and so is the pesto sauce. I once made two thousand
of these for an event sponsored by the James Beard Foundation,
and people devoured every one of them in less than two hours.

1 ½ pounds Lemon-Dill Pasta dough (page 100)
1 cup softened goat cheese
1 pound freshly ground lamb
1 teaspoon olive oil
Salt and pepper
Egg wash (1 egg beaten with 1 tablespoon water) for pasta
Basil and Pine Nut Sauce (recipe follows)

*D*ivide the dough in half and roll out each piece into a sheet about ⅛ inch thick. With a round cutter 1 inch in diameter, mark circles on the sheet about 1 inch apart, making between 50 and 60 marks. Sauté the ground lamb in the olive oil for approximately 2 minutes. Put ½ teaspoon each of goat cheese and ground lamb, seasoned to taste, on each round mark. Paint egg wash around the inside of each circle. Place the second sheet of pasta over the first sheet. Using a round, 1 ½-inch cutter, cut the pasta into circular ravioli. Seal the edges with a fork. Sprinkle a baking sheet lightly with cornmeal or flour to prevent the pasta from sticking and place the ravioli on the pan. Set the ravioli aside, covered, while you make the sauce.

To cook the ravioli, drop them into boiling water for between 7 and 9 minutes or until they are *al dente*; drain, and simmer in the sauce for 2 or 3 minutes.

Serves 8

BASIL & PINE NUT SAUCE

1 cup olive oil
½ cup fresh basil leaves
¼ cup pine nuts
Salt and pepper, to taste

*P*lace the oil, basil, pine nuts, and salt and pepper in blender; purée the ingredients and set aside.

Fettuccine *with*

Walnuts & Avocado ♥

Few people would expect to find avocados on a low-fat menu because
they are mostly fat. What they contain is monounsaturated fat
(the kind that is found in olive oil), which helps to lower cholesterol levels.
They also add a little richness to this recipe. If you are concerned about
cholesterol, substitute a pasta that has been made without eggs.
If fettuccine noodles are not available, use any dried pasta.

2 tablespoons olive oil
$\frac{1}{4}$ cup sherry vinegar
$\frac{1}{2}$ cup fresh chopped basil
2 tablespoons chopped green onions
$\frac{1}{4}$ cup diced green bell pepper
$\frac{1}{2}$ cup sun-dried tomatoes
2 tablespoons chopped walnuts
1 California avocado, pitted, peeled, and diced
1 pound dried *fettuccine*

In a large bowl, combine the olive oil, vinegar, basil, green
onions, bell pepper, sun-dried tomatoes, walnuts, and half of
the diced avocado. Toss the ingredients well so that they are
evenly coated with the oil and vinegar.

Cook the pasta in boiling water approximately 3 minutes
or until *al dente*. Drain the pasta, turn it into the salad bowl,
and mix with the tossed vegetables. Garnish the pasta with
the remaining diced avocado.

Serves 6

MAIN COURSES

Fish & Seafood

I think that if you asked any French chef which food he preferred to cook, he'd most probably say seafood. There is such variety in the species, the textures, the tastes, and the seasonality. Seafood, because it is generally delicately flavored, takes very well to everything from butter and cream to garlic and pepper.

Obviously the Southwest is not prime territory for seafood, but we bring in the best from the Pacific and the Atlantic.

SOUTHWESTERN MUSSELS

This is a great dish to make for a large crowd—everyone can dig in—
and it's simple to prepare. When choosing mussels make sure that the
shells are tightly closed or snap shut when tapped. If mussels feel heavy,
they may be full of sand and should be avoided. If they feel light and
loose when shaken, the mussel is dead. Smaller mussels are usually
more tender than larger ones are. Use mussels within
a day or two of buying them because they are very perishable.

2 cups dry white wine
½ cup chopped shallots
½ cup tomato, peeled, seeded, and diced
½ cup heavy cream
⅓ cup chopped cilantro
Salt and pepper
48 fresh medium-sized mussels, brushed and cleaned
4 tablespoons butter, cut into ½-inch cubes

Combine the wine, shallots, tomato, cream, and cilantro. Add salt and pepper to taste. Bring the mixture to a boil, then immerse the mussels into it. Cover the pan and allow the mussels to boil for approximately 1 minute. Remove the pan from heat and take out the mussels. They should all be open; throw away those that are still closed. Set the mussels aside, return the liquid to the pan, and bring it to a boil again. Cook the liquid for approximately 2 or 3 minutes to reduce it to about 1 cup. Adjust the seasoning by adding salt and pepper to taste. Slowly add the butter until it is incorporated. Serve the mussels in a deep dish with the sauce poured over them.

Serves 4

GRILLED SKEWERED SEAFOOD *with*

DILL MAYONNAISE

This is a great dish for a summer barbecue because it's simple and fast.
The fish used can be changed according to your own taste.
The dill mayonnaise makes a refreshing sauce. Remember that,
if you are outdoors in the heat, be sure to keep the mayonnaise cold,
preferably in the refrigerator, bringing it out just before serving.

6 wood skewers
6 medium shrimp
6 ounces 'ahi tuna
6 ounces salmon
6 ounces swordfish
6 large scallops
3 tablespoons olive oil
Salt and pepper
3 tablespoons chopped dill
Dill Mayonnaise (recipe follows)

Soak the skewers in water while preparing the seafood.

Peel and devein the shrimp. Cut the tuna, salmon, and swordfish into 1-ounce pieces. Thread the pieces of seafood onto the skewers and brush the fish with olive oil. Sprinkle with salt and pepper, to taste, and with the dill. Grill the seafood over high heat for approximately 5 minutes on each side. Serve hot with dill mayonnaise.

Serves 6

DILL MAYONNAISE

1 egg yolk
1 teaspoon Dijon mustard
Salt and pepper
½ cup salad oil
1 tablespoon chopped dill

In a mixing bowl blend the egg yolk, mustard, salt, and pepper. Very slowly whisk in the oil. Add the chopped dill.

Makes ½ cup

STEAMED SHRIMP & SCALLOPS *with* GINGER, BASIL, & ORANGE♥

The supremely talented Martin Yan, who hosts the PBS-TV show "Yan Can Cook,"
took me to Chinatown in San Francisco one day, and I was amazed at the number
of seafood dishes steamed in bamboo—a technique I thought was very healthful
and one that retained the delicate flavor of the seafood. When I got back to
Phoenix I experimented, added some western herbs and seasonings, and came
up with this luscious but very light shellfish recipe. It's great at any time of
the year and works with any shellfish—choose whatever is best in the market.

2 oranges ✦ 8 large scallops
8 medium shrimp, peeled and deveined
2 teaspoons peeled, grated ginger
2 tablespoons chopped basil
5 tablespoons olive oil ✦ Salt and pepper
1 cup white wine ✦ 1 teaspoon chopped shallot
1 tablespoon sherry vinegar

Zest, peel, and quarter the oranges. Place the scallops and
shrimp in a bamboo steamer. Add the ginger, basil, orange
zest, 2 tablespoons of the olive oil, and a dash of salt and pepper. In a steamer pan or a skillet that will accommodate the
bamboo steamer, place the white wine, chopped shallot, and
orange slices. Bring the mixture to a boil and steam the
shrimp and scallops over it for approximately 5 minutes or
until the seafood is cooked through.

Serve with a green salad dressed with a tablespoon of
sherry wine vinegar and the remaining 3 tablespoons oil.

Serves 4

BAKED JOHN DORY *with*
CILANTRO CREAM

John Dory is a delicate, mild fish that is delicious grilled or sautéed.
If John Dory is not available, substitute another
mildly flavored fish such as halibut or swordfish.

4 John Dory fillets, each weighing about 6 ounces
½ cup dry white wine
½ cup chopped shallots
1 cup heavy cream
1 cup chopped cilantro, plus extra leaves for garnish
Salt and pepper
½ cup diced tomato, for garnish

Preheat the oven to 500°F. Place the John Dory fillets in a deep baking dish. Combine the white wine, shallots, cream, and chopped cilantro and pour the mixture over the fish. Add salt and pepper if desired. Bake the fish uncovered for approximately 7 minutes. Remove the dish from the oven and place the fish on serving plates.

Pour the liquid from the baking dish into a blender and blend until it is creamy. Strain the liquid through a fine sieve and season to taste with salt and pepper. Serve the fish with sauce on top and garnished with diced tomato and cilantro leaves.

Serves 4

GRILLED LOBSTER *with*

YELLOW HOT CHILES

*This is one of our most popular items and has been on the menu since
we opened. The yellow hot chile, also known as* guëro, *can vary in taste
from medium to hot. People love them with the sweet flesh of the lobster.
When buying lobsters, be sure that they are still alive because
bacteria multiply quickly in dead lobsters. When you pick up
the lobster, the tail should curl under. If stored in fresh water,
they will die, so plan to cook them the day you buy them.*

4 lobsters, 1 pound each

Olive oil

2 shallots, peeled and chopped

8 medium-sized *guëros* (yellow hot *chile* peppers),
roasted, peeled, and seeded (page 266)

1 cup dry white wine

⅓ cup heavy cream

1 ½ cups (3 sticks) unsalted butter, cut into ½-inch cubes

1 teaspoon chopped basil

Quarter of a fresh lemon

Salt and pepper

Cut the lobsters in half lengthwise and remove the stomach sack, which is in the head, and the intestinal vein, which runs down the length of the body. Brush the lobster with olive oil and grill them, meat-side down first, over a very hot fire for between 7 and 8 minutes. Turn them over and grill them, shell-side down, for 5 minutes. (If a grill is not available, steam or poach the lobsters for 7 minutes each.) Crack open the claws and set the lobsters aside.

To make the sauce, combine the shallots, 4 of the *chiles* (which have been quartered), and the wine. Bring the mixture to a boil and reduce it until there is no liquid left. This will take approximately 5 minutes. Add the cream and simmer for approximately 2 minutes. Remove the pan from the heat and whisk in the butter in increments. Strain the sauce, and add the basil and the juice from the quarter lemon. Add salt and pepper to taste.

Pour the sauce over the lobster and garnish with the remaining yellow *chiles*.

Serves 4

GRILLED SALMON *with*
JALAPEÑO HONEY GLAZE♥

Salmon is one fish that can easily stand up to a sweetness in the sauce. The glaze in this recipe gets deep down into the flesh and makes it succulent and smoky. The jalapeño *gives it some bite.*

2 pounds fresh salmon fillets
Salt and pepper
2 teaspoons chopped *jalapeño* pepper
¼ cup honey

Cut the salmon into six 5-ounce portions. Season the fish with salt and pepper. Combine the chopped *jalapeño* and the honey and set this glaze aside. Spray a medium-hot grill with nonfat cooking spray and grill the salmon for approximately 4 minutes on each side or until it is firm in the center. (If a grill is not available, the fish may be sautéed; it will take the same time to cook.) During the last 2 minutes of cooking, brush the uppermost side with the *jalapeño* and honey glaze and do not turn the fish over after that or the glaze will stick to the grill.

Serves 6

GRILLED SALMON *with* TOMATILLO CREAM

A wonderful dish in which the lemony flavor and tartness
of the tomatillos complements the succulent flesh of the salmon.
At Vincent's we serve this with black bean salad (page 34).

4 salmon fillets, each weighing about 6 ounces
2 tablespoons olive oil ❧ Salt and pepper
Tomatillo Cream (recipe follows)

Make the *tomatillo* cream first and set it aside.

Brush the salmon fillets with the olive oil and sprinkle them with salt and pepper. Grill the fish over hot coals for approximately 2 minutes on each side.

To serve, garnish the fillets with whole *tomatillos* and pour some of the *tomatillo* cream around each piece of salmon.

Serves 4

TOMATILLO CREAM

12 medium *tomatillos* ❧ 1 cup heavy cream
Salt and pepper ❧ 1 tablespoon butter

Blanch the *tomatillos* in boiling water, peel off the husks, and remove the stems from 8 of the *tomatillos*. Reserve the remaining 4 for garnishing the salmon. Cut the 8 *tomatillos* into quarters and heat them, with the cream and the salt and pepper, for about 3 or 4 minutes. Purée the mixture in a blender until it is creamy and taste for seasoning. Strain the purée through a medium-fine sieve, return it to the saucepan, reheat it, and whisk in the butter. Continue cooking the sauce, stirring all the while, for 2 or 3 minutes longer. Keep warm until ready to serve.

Blue Corn–Crusted Salmon *with* Citrus & Cilantro Salsa♥

Less elaborate than it sounds, this dish of salmon fillets
is simply dusted with cornmeal for the crust.

4 salmon fillets, each weighing about 6 ounces
1 tablespoon olive oil
Salt and pepper
2 tablespoons blue cornmeal*
1 tablespoon chopped cilantro
1 teaspoon lemon juice
Citrus and Cilantro Salsa (recipe follows)

Make the citrus and cilantro salsa 2 hours before serving time to allow the flavors to blend.

Preheat the oven to 400°F. Place the salmon fillets on a baking sheet pan and brush them with olive oil. Season with salt and pepper. Dust the tops with the blue cornmeal. Bake the salmon for between 12 and 15 minutes and then place the pan under a preheated broiler for just a few seconds to form a crust on the fish.

Sprinkle the salmon with cilantro and lemon juice and serve with citrus and cilantro salsa.

Serves 4

*Substitute yellow cornmeal if blue is not available.

CITRUS & CILANTRO SALSA

4 mandarin oranges, peeled and sliced
2 tablespoons chopped cilantro
1 tablespoon finely diced red onion
1 tablespoon finely diced yellow (or red or green) bell pepper
1 teaspoon finely diced *jalapeño* pepper
1 *tomatillo,* diced
½ cup Triple Sec liqueur
Salt and pepper

Mix the mandarin oranges, cilantro, onion, peppers, and *tomatillo* together, stir in the liqueur, and season to taste. Set aside for 2 hours before serving to allow time for the flavors to blend.

Makes 2 cups

Salmon in Parchment

with Ginger & Lime

*Grilled salmon is excellent, but the fish also comes off well when
cooked in parchment paper, a method in France called* en papillote.
*As steam builds during the cooking process, the paper will puff up.
Before serving, slit the paper to release the steam and then peel back
the paper to reveal the food. Many things are prepared in this manner,
but it works particularly well with fish because the fish
stays moist and flavorful without needing a lot of oils or fats.
And the aromas coming out of the little envelopes are incredibly good.*

4 medium carrots, julienned

4 medium leeks, julienned

4 small stalks celery, julienned

4 salmon fillets, 6 ounces each

4 pieces parchment paper, each measuring 8 by 12 inches

4 tablespoons black olive purée or use canned black olives
that have been puréed in the blender until smooth

¼ cup tomato, peeled, seeded, and diced

4 teaspoons grated fresh ginger or 1 teaspoon ground ginger

4 tablespoons chopped fresh basil or 1 teaspoon dried basil

4 teaspoons lime juice

Cilantro *Beurre Blanc* (page 268)

Preheat the oven to 400°F.

Blanch the carrots, leeks, and celery together by dropping
them into boiling water and removing them when the water
returns to a boil. Place each salmon fillet in the center of a
piece of parchment paper and spread 1 tablespoon of the olive purée over each piece of fish. Top the purée with some of

118

the blanched vegetables, diced tomato, ginger, basil, and lime juice. Fold the two sides of the paper over the fish and its topping. Pick up the two ends and fold them over together, making a neat seam. Bake the parcels for approximately 15 minutes.

Just before serving, make a small slit in the parchment and serve the fish hot, with cilantro *beurre blanc*.

Serves 4

Salmon in Puff Pastry

*When you really want to show off your culinary talents,
make this—it's a real showpiece. You can make the dish
either in individual portions or smaller, in hors d'oeuvre sizes,
and you can assemble everything in advance.*

2 tablespoons olive oil
1 cup chopped basil
1 cup red bell pepper, cored and diced
1 cup green bell pepper, cored and diced
1 cup yellow bell pepper, cored and diced
Salt and pepper
2 tablespoons lemon juice
2 pieces fillet of salmon, 1½ pounds each
8 ounces salmon fillet, for the mousse
2 cups whipping cream
1½ pounds puff pastry (half the recipe on page 223)*
1 egg, beaten with 1 tablespoon water, to make an egg wash

Combine the oil, basil, bell peppers, salt and pepper to taste, and lemon juice and marinate the pieces of fillet of salmon in the mixture overnight.

To make the salmon mousse, use a food processor bowl and blade which have been chilled in the refrigerator until they are very cold. Process the 8 ounces of salmon fillet with 1 teaspoon of salt and the cream for between 3 and 4 minutes by pulsing the machine on and off. Strain the mixture through a sieve and refrigerate it.

*If you do not wish to make your own puff pastry, Pepperidge Farm sells an adequate version, to be found in the freezer cases in most supermarkets. Or puff pastry dough may be ordered from a restaurant.

Roll out 2 pieces of puff pastry (approximately 12 ounces each) into 2 rectangular sheets measuring 16 by 8 inches and ⅛ inch thick.

Preheat the oven to 375°F. Remove the whole fillets from the marinade and wipe them off. Line a baking tray with parchment paper, place 1 of the sheets of pastry on the paper, and place 1 marinated fillet of salmon in the center of the pastry. Spread the mousse evenly over the top of the fillet. Cover the mousse with the other fillet and cover that with the second rectangle of pastry. Seal the 2 sheets of pastry with egg wash. With a knife, cut away excess dough and shape the pastry into the form of a fish. Brush the top with egg wash and bake for 25 minutes, or until golden brown. Slice the pastry with an electric knife and serve it hot.

Serves 8

BROILED SALMON *with* WHOLE-GRAIN MUSTARD & SAGE CRUST♥

This dish is succulent because the mustard crust keeps
the fish moist and tender. Sage has a slightly bitter flavor,
so adjust the amount you use to your own taste.

4 boned salmon fillets, each weighing 6 ounces
1 tablespoon olive oil
4 tablespoons whole-grain mustard
4 tablespoons chopped fresh sage or 1 tablespoon dried sage

𝒫lace the salmon fillets on a baking sheet and brush them with olive oil on both sides. Mix mustard and sage together. Coat the top of each fillet with the mustard mixture. Broil the salmon for approximately 12 to 15 minutes or until the mustard coating is lightly browned. Serve hot.

Serves 4

Grilled Sea Bass *with* Chimayó Chile

In this recipe the chile-flavored sea bass may be served as fillets or, more dramatically, as the whole fish.

4 sea bass fillets, each weighing about 6 ounces,
or 2 whole sea bass, weighing between 1½ and 2 pounds each
1 tablespoon olive oil
1 tablespoon medium-hot pure Chimayó *chile* powder
Salt and pepper
1 lemon, sliced into 4 wedges

For fillets, be sure that the skin is attached to the fillets, but that no scales remain. Brush the fillets on both sides with olive oil. Dust with *chile* powder, salt, and pepper. Grill the fish over a very hot grill for approximately 2 minutes on each side.

For whole fish, scale and dress the sea bass. Brush the fish with olive oil and sprinkle them lightly with *chile* powder, salt, and pepper. Grill the sea bass over very hot coals for approximately 4 minutes on each side.

Set the fish aside for 3 to 4 minutes before serving and garnish with a lemon wedge on each plate.

Serves 4

Grilled Halibut *with* Citrus Sauce

A simply grilled piece of fish provides the perfect foil for the subtle sauce.

4 halibut fillets, each weighing about 8 ounces
1 tablespoon olive oil
Salt and pepper
Citrus Sauce (recipe follows)

Make the sauce first and set it aside, keeping it warm.

Brush the fillets with olive oil. Add salt and pepper and grill the fish for approximately 3 minutes on each side. Serve hot with ¼ cup citrus sauce for each serving.

Serves 4

Citrus Sauce

1 cup white wine
1 cup white wine vinegar
1 cup orange juice
1 tablespoon lime juice
1 tablespoon lemon juice
1 tablespoon chopped shallots
1 tablespoon heavy cream
1 pound (4 sticks) unsalted butter, softened
1 tablespoon orange rind, grated and blanched
1 tablespoon lime rind, grated and blanched
1 tablespoon lemon rind, grated and blanched
Salt and pepper

Put the wine, vinegar, citrus juices, and shallots in a skillet and reduce over moderate heat until the liquid is completely gone. Whisk in the cream and the softened butter, 4 tablespoons at a time. Strain the sauce and add the orange, lime, and lemon rinds. Serve the sauce hot.

Makes 2 cups

Grilled Swordfish or Salmon

with Ginger, Lime, & Cilantro Sauce

I like the combination of the peppery ginger and the tartness of the lime for either of these fish. Use a mature ginger that has smooth skin and is not wrinkled. Make sure that it has a spicy fragrance and is juicy inside when cut open.

4 slices ginger, peeled and sliced ❧ 1 teaspoon chopped shallots
1 cup white wine ❧ 1 tablespoon grated ginger ❧ ⅓ cup heavy cream
1½ cups (3 sticks) butter, cut into ½-inch cubes
Juice of 2 limes (3 tablespoons) ❧ 1 tablespoon chopped cilantro
Salt and pepper ❧ 4 slices swordfish or salmon, 8 ounces each

*B*rush the slices of ginger with olive oil and place them on a grill, cooking until they are marked golden brown.

To make the sauce, combine the shallots, wine, and grated ginger and bring the mixture to a boil. Reduce until there is no liquid left. Add the cream and bring the mixture to a boil again. Whisk in the butter in small increments. Take the pan off the heat and add the lime juice, cilantro, and salt and pepper to taste. Set the sauce aside in a warm place.

Season the swordfish or salmon with salt and pepper and grill the fish over high heat for approximately 4 minutes on each side. Top each piece with a slice of grilled ginger, pour some sauce around the fish, and serve hot.

Variation
This recipe may also be used for salmon.

Serves 4

Grilled 'Ahi Tuna *with* Grilled Scallions♥

The sweet, tart flavor of papaya and the pungent flavor of cilantro make a beautiful accompaniment for this 'ahi tuna. The flavor of the fish comes through best when it is cooked medium rare, although many people like it when it is barely warm on the inside.

2½ pounds 'ahi tuna
2 tablespoons olive oil
Salt and freshly ground black pepper
12 whole scallions
Papaya and Cilantro Salsa (page 83)
Cilantro, for garnish

Cut the tuna into 6 portions, each ½ inch thick. Rub both sides of the tuna with olive oil and season with salt and pepper. Arrange the tuna on a hot grill, or in a sauté pan, and cook it for approximately 3 minutes on each side. The tuna is served medium rare.

Blanch the scallions in boiling water for 30 seconds; remove them and season with salt and pepper. Grill the scallions for approximately 1 minute on each side, or sauté them over medium-high heat in 1 teaspoon olive oil.

To serve, place a slice of tuna on each plate and arrange the grilled scallions on top of the fish making an X. Place 1 tablespoon of papaya cilantro salsa over the X and garnish with a sprig of cilantro.

Serves 6

GRILLED MAHI-MAHI *with*
RED BELL PEPPER CREAM,
TOMATILLO, & CORN SALSA

*Mahi-mahi, also called dorado, is the dolphinfish
and is not to be confused with the true dolphin, which is a mammal.
Grilling is one of the best ways of cooking this fish.
A* tomatillo, *also called* tomate verde, tomate de cáscara, *and* fresadilla
*in Mexico, resembles a small green tomato but is covered with a papery
husk. They are generally used when they are green and very firm, but
sometimes they are left to ripen to a yellow color. The taste is similar to
that of a tomato but there are perceptible tones of citrus and apples.
They are usually found in Latin-American markets and in some
supermarkets. When purchasing* tomatillos, *choose fruit that has dry,
tight-fitting husks. Remove the husks and wash the fruit
thoroughly before using it. They can also be purchased canned
(sometimes called* tomatillo entero *or* tomatillo verde)
but the fresh fruit has much more flavor.

1 ½ pounds trimmed mahi-mahi, cut into 6 slices
¼ cup olive oil
Salt and pepper
Tomatillo and Corn Salsa (recipe follows)
Red Bell Pepper Cream (recipe follows)

*P*repare the salsa first, preferably at least 2 hours ahead of
time to allow the flavors to blend. Shortly before grilling the
fish, prepare the red bell pepper cream and set it aside, keeping it hot.

Rub the mahi-mahi with olive oil and season both sides

with salt and black pepper. Grill the fish on a medium-hot grill for approximately 4 minutes on each side. (To sauté the fish if a grill is not available, put a small quantity of olive oil in a sauté pan and cook the mahi-mahi over medium-high heat for approximately 4 minutes on each side.)

To serve, pour a pool of red bell pepper cream onto each plate and put a slice of mahi-mahi on top. Garnish each slice of fish with the salsa.

Serves 6

Tomatillo & Corn Salsa

10 medium-sized *tomatillos*
2 Anaheim (New Mexico) *chiles*
1 ear corn or ½ cup frozen corn kernels
2 cloves garlic, minced
3 tablespoons chopped basil
2 tablespoons olive oil
1 tablespoon sherry vinegar
Salt and pepper

Blanch the *tomatillos* in boiling water and remove the husks. Cut them into very small dice. Split the *chiles* in half, remove the stem and seeds, and dice finely. Boil the ear of corn for 5 minutes, cool it in ice water, and remove the kernels. Mix the *tomatillos, chiles,* and corn. Add the garlic, basil, oil, and vinegar. Season to taste and refrigerate.

Makes 2 cups

RED BELL PEPPER CREAM

2 red bell peppers, stemmed, seeded, and coarsely chopped
2 cloves garlic, minced
1 whole shallot, minced
½ cup white wine
¼ cup white wine vinegar
1 cup heavy cream
½ cup (1 stick) unsalted butter, cut into ½-inch cubes
Salt and white pepper

Combine the peppers, garlic, shallot, white wine, and vinegar in a saucepan. Bring the mixture to a boil and then simmer it for approximately 15 minutes. Purée the mixture in a blender until it is smooth and return it to the saucepan. Add the cream, place over low heat, and simmer the mixture for 10 minutes. Slowly whisk in the butter in increments and adjust the seasoning with salt and white pepper. Strain the sauce through a fine sieve and keep it hot.

Makes 1½ cups

Poultry

Of all the meats available to a cook, chicken is by far the most versatile—not only because it is the most readily available but also because it takes so well to a variety of seasonings and of techniques, from roasting to stewing to frying. Most American chickens haven't the rich flavor of European chickens—though they have more fat. If you can find so-called free-range chickens that are not raised by the millions in small coops, you'll notice that they do have more flavor. They may, however, be a little less tender. I also love to work with duck, a fattier, tougher-fleshed bird that certainly does not lack flavor.

GRILLED CHICKEN *with*

WILD MUSHROOM CREAM SAUCE

These days the definition of "wild" mushrooms is a little blurred when many of us can buy a selection of once-exotic mushrooms in the neighborhood market, a much safer source of supply for the neophyte mushroom fancier. For their own protection, gatherers of the untamed mushroom to be found in the woods should be carefully chaperoned or thoroughly knowledgeable. For the rest of us, the term "wild" is merely a catch-all to describe any mushroom other than the domesticated, white button mushroom that, interestingly, the authors of Larousse Gastronomique *consider to be "anyway, one of the best species."*

4 boneless chicken breasts with skin on, each weighing about 6 ounces
2 tablespoons olive oil
Salt and pepper
Wild Mushroom Cream Sauce (recipe follows)

*P*repare the sauce first.

Brush the chicken with olive oil on both sides and season with salt and pepper to taste. Grill (or sauté) the chicken over a hot fire for approximately 7 minutes on each side. Set aside for a few minutes before serving, remove the skin, and serve the chicken with wild mushroom cream sauce.

Serves 4

Wild Mushroom Cream Sauce

1 pound morels, *chanterelles, shiitake,* Portobello,
or oyster mushrooms or a combination
4 tablespoons (½ stick) butter
1 tablespoon chopped shallot
¼ cup dry white wine
1 cup heavy cream
Salt and pepper
2 tablespoons chopped parsley

Wash and pat dry the mushrooms, coarsely chopping the larger ones. Sauté them in hot butter for approximately 4 or 5 minutes or until the butter has been absorbed. Add the chopped shallot. Then add the wine and reduce until the liquid is completely gone. Add the cream and salt and pepper to taste and simmer the sauce for approximately 2 minutes, stirring constantly. Just before serving, add the chopped parsley.

133

Sautéed Chicken Breast *with* Lime Beurre Blanc

The sauce for this recipe is a variation on the traditional beurre blanc, *but the lime juice is delicious with the chicken.*

½ recipe Lime *Beurre Blanc* (page 268)
4 boneless chicken breasts with skin, each weighing about 6 ounces
Salt and pepper
2 tablespoons olive oil
2 tablespoons lime zest, for garnish

Make the sauce first (be sure that the lime juice is well blended so that acid doesn't make the sauce separate) and keep it warm in a double boiler or a water bath until you are ready to serve.

Season the chicken with salt and pepper. Heat the olive oil in a sauté pan until it is very hot. Cook the chicken for approximately 7 or 8 minutes on each side, but not so long that it dries out. Remove the chicken skin just before serving. Serve with lime *beurre blanc* and grated lime zest on top.

Serves 4

GRILLED CHICKEN &
BELL PEPPER SKEWERS♥

A straightforward, delicious combination,
this dish can be made even more colorful toward
the end of summer, when bell peppers of various colors—
orange, ivory, purple, and even chocolate—
come on the market.

4 wood or bamboo skewers, about 12 inches long,
soaked in water to prevent their burning
4 boneless chicken breasts, each weighing about 6 ounces
1 medium red bell pepper
1 medium yellow bell pepper
1 medium green bell pepper
1 small red onion
2 tablespoons olive oil
Salt and pepper
Juice of 1 lemon
2 tablespoons chopped basil

While the skewers are soaking, prepare the chicken and vegetables. Cut the chicken breasts into cubes, dice the peppers, quarter the onion, and separate the quarters into layers.

On each skewer, alternate chicken, bell pepper cubes, and onion layers. Brush each skewer with olive oil and season with salt and pepper. Grill the skewers over a hot grill for approximately 2 or 3 minutes on each side. Serve with lemon juice and chopped basil sprinkled on top.

Serves 4

Grilled Chicken Breast *with* Jícama & Sweet Peppers & Sherry Vinegar Sauce

Jícama, certainly not to be found in traditional French cooking, is too good to ignore. The flavor is subtle and slightly sweet; the texture is crunchy, softer than carrot, harder than celery. Be sure not to overcook it.

4 boneless chicken breasts, weighing about 6 ounces each
Salt and pepper
5 tablespoons olive oil
1 small *jícama,* peeled and julienned
1 red bell pepper, julienned
1 yellow bell pepper, julienned
1 green bell pepper, julienned
Sherry Vinegar Sauce (recipe follows)

Season the chicken breasts with salt and pepper, brush them with 1 tablespoon of the olive oil, and grill them for between 6 and 8 minutes on each side. Remove the breasts from the grill and set them aside, keeping them warm.

Heat the remaining 4 tablespoons of olive oil and sauté the *jícama* in it for approximately 2 minutes. Remove the *jícama* and in the same skillet, sauté the bell peppers, also for 2 minutes.

Place the *jícama* on a plate with the breast of chicken on top. Arrange bell peppers around the sides and serve hot with sherry vinegar sauce.

Serves 4

VINCENT'S COOKBOOK

SHERRY VINEGAR SAUCE

½ cup sherry vinegar
1 tablespoon chicken glaze (page 265) or chicken stock
4 tablespoons olive oil
Salt and pepper

Boil the vinegar in a saucepan over high heat until it has reduced by half. Add the chicken glaze or stock and olive oil. Add salt and pepper to taste and set the sauce aside over low heat to keep warm.

Grilled Chicken Breast

with Garlic ♥

This simple dish of chicken breast reminds me of bistro food, which I like. The grilled garlic served with it is mild but still very flavorful.

6 heads of garlic
6 chicken breasts with skin on, each weighing about 6 ounces
Salt and pepper
3 tablespoons olive oil
⅓ cup chopped cilantro
3 garlic cloves, peeled and minced

Grill the garlic heads for approximately 30 minutes over medium heat, turning them frequently. (Lacking a grill, bake them for 45 minutes at 275°F.)

Season the chicken with salt and pepper to taste and grill on a hot grill for approximately 10 minutes on each side. Set aside. (If a grill is not available, the chicken breasts may be roasted in a 450°F oven for approximately the same length of time.)

Mix the olive oil, cilantro, and minced garlic, heat until warm, and pour the sauce over the grilled chicken breasts. Slice the root ends from the garlic and serve the heads alongside.

Serves 6

Mesquite-Grilled Chicken *with* Chipotle & Apple Chutney

The marriage of chile peppers and fruit is the basis for so much southwestern cooking, and I find apples particularly versatile for this kind of dish. Try to grill over a hardwood fire. We use mesquite, which can be purchased as chunks or briquets, but other woods, too, will impart a wonderful flavor.

4 chicken thighs, weighing 5 to 6 ounces each
1 tablespoon olive oil
Salt and pepper
Chipotle and Apple Chutney (recipe follows)

Make the chutney first, in time for it to have cooled down to room temperature before being served.

Rub the chicken with the olive oil and season with salt and pepper to taste. Grill the chicken over a hot mesquite fire for approximately 20 minutes, turning 2 or 3 times. Serve the chicken hot with the *chipotle* and apple chutney at room temperature.

Serves 4

CHIPOTLE & APPLE CHUTNEY

½ cup sherry vinegar

¼ cup granulated sugar

½ cup brown sugar

1 Granny Smith apple, cored, but not peeled, and finely diced

3 Anaheim (New Mexico) *chiles,* roasted, peeled, seeded, and diced (see page 266)

1 teaspoon puréed *chile chipotle en adobo* (canned *chipotle chiles* in adobo sauce)
or 2 teaspoons dried *chipotle chiles* pulverized in a blender

1 teaspoon chopped garlic

Combine the vinegar, sugars, apple, *chiles,* and garlic
in a saucepan and bring the mixture to a boil. Reduce
the heat to low and cook until thick, about 10 minutes.
Serve the chutney at room temperature.

Makes 1 cup

Marinated Chile Chicken *with*
Pine Nut & Cilantro Butter

*Marinating the chicken helps to tenderize it and
the pine nuts and cilantro work well with the* chile.

1 tablespoon olive oil
1 tablespoon lemon juice
1 tablespoon pure *chipotle chile* powder
¼ cup plus 1 tablespoon chopped cilantro
4 boneless chicken breasts with the skin on, each weighing about 6 ounces
8 tablespoons (1 stick) butter
¼ cup pine nuts
Salt and pepper

Mix together the olive oil, lemon juice, *chile* powder, and
1 tablespoon of the chopped cilantro to make a marinade.
Marinate the chicken breasts in this mixture for at least 2
hours in the refrigerator. Remove the chicken and save the
marinade. Grill, or sauté, the chicken over medium heat for
between 6 and 8 minutes on each side or until it is cooked
through. Set aside, keeping it warm, while you make the
sauce. Just before serving, remove the skin.

In a skillet over low heat, blend the reserved marinade, the
butter, pine nuts, remaining ¼ cup cilantro, and add salt and
pepper to taste. When the butter has melted, serve the sauce
hot over the cooked chicken.

Serves 4

Duck Confit *with* Garlic

Duck confit *is something I have been making for years. It is one of the glories of French cuisine and, I have discovered, it goes spectacularly well with the pronounced flavors of Southwest spices. I learned to make* confit *during my apprenticeship in the south of France, and although it takes a while for the* confit *to cure, the actual preparation and cooking is easy and simple.* Confit *refers to the preparation technique. The duck is cooked in its own fat and left to cool. The fat rises to the top of the meat and hardens, forming a tight seal that preserves the meat beautifully and enriches the flavor. It becomes very tender and will keep for several weeks when stored this way. The meat can be served alone as a main dish or shredded and used in many different ways. We use it for pizza topping, in salads, to fill* tamales, *and on* quesadillas.

2 ducks, each weighing between 4 and 5 pounds
4 heads garlic, cut in half
2 sprigs thyme or 2 teaspoons dried thyme
2 sprigs rosemary or 2 teaspoons dried rosemary
2 bay leaves
2 cups dry white wine
¼ cup coarse kosher salt

Have your butcher bone the duck breast and legs, leaving the skin on but removing as much fat as possible. Save the fat and render it for 1 hour over low heat. Strain the fat and refrigerate it.

Place the duck pieces in a stainless-steel bowl, add the garlic, herbs, wine, and salt and marinate the duck for 36 hours in the refrigerator.

Preheat the oven to 225°F. Using an ovenproof pan that

may be heated on the top of the stove, melt the reserved duck fat. Add the pieces of duck with the marinade, making sure that they are covered by the fat, and bake the duck, uncovered, for 4½ hours.

As a main course we serve half a duck breast and a leg, accompanied by Anasazi beans or sautéed or grilled potatoes. When the *confit* is to be used as a topping or filling, we scrape off the excess fat, remove the bones, and shred the meat. The *confit,* well covered with its own fat, will keep for several weeks in a cool, dark place or may be frozen.

Serves 4 as a main course; makes 8 cups duck meat when shredded

GRILLED CORNISH GAME HEN *with*

CHESTNUTS & CRANBERRIES

A wonderful holiday alternative to turkey, Cornish hens don't
take much time to roast and there is no need to carve them.
For those with big appetites, a whole Cornish hen is a serving,
but the plumper varieties of the hen will serve two.

4 Cornish game hens, each weighing about 18 ounces
6 tablespoons olive oil
Salt and pepper
12 canned, peeled whole chestnuts
½ cup fresh or frozen cranberries

Brush the Cornish hens with 4 tablespoons of the olive oil and season with salt and pepper. Grill the birds over a hot grill for approximately 7 minutes on each side. If a grill is not available, bake the hens in the oven at 450°F for 15 minutes. Remove and set aside.

In a skillet over medium-high heat, sauté the chestnuts in the remaining 2 tablespoons olive oil for between 2 and 3 minutes. Add the cranberries and continue to sauté for another 2 minutes, until the chestnuts are golden brown. Serve hot.

Serves 4

Lamb

The United States produces some of the best lamb in the world, yet Americans eat so little of it—only about one pound per person each year, compared to sixty-six pounds of beef and fifty-three pounds of pork! Lamb has a marvelous flavor and, if cooked medium-rare or at least pink, it is tremendously juicy and tender. Young lamb tastes better, however, if you cook it more, to medium.

LAMB CHOPS *with* HERBS & GARLIC

*At Vincent's we frequently serve these lamb chops
with eggplant and goat cheese* timbales *because the
combination of taste and texture is so good.*

4 cloves garlic, peeled
4 racks of lamb, each weighing approximately 14 ounces
½ cup olive oil
1 cup chicken glaze or chicken stock (page 264)
2 sprigs rosemary or 2 teaspoons dried rosemary
2 sprigs thyme or 2 teaspoons dried thyme
Salt and pepper

Simmer the garlic cloves in water until they are tender, about
15 to 20 minutes. Set aside. If you are serving them, prepare
the eggplant *timbales* (page 184). While they are baking, grill
the lamb and make the sauce.

Cut the racks into chops and brush them with 2 tablespoons of olive oil. Sauté or grill the chops over very high
heat for approximately 1 minute on each side; they will be
medium rare.

Make a sauce by mixing the chicken glaze, the remaining
olive oil, rosemary, thyme, and blanched garlic cloves. (If using fresh rosemary and thyme, remove sprigs prior to serving.) Bring the mixture to a boil and then reduce it to a simmer
to keep warm until you are ready to serve.

Serves 4

BROCHETTES OF LAMB

Brochettes of lamb may be prepared in advance, set aside, and then grilled at the last minute. Served with a side dish of wild rice and fresh corn, and a salad, these become part of a great outdoor barbecue.

4 bamboo or metal skewers, about 6 inches long
1 ½ pounds boneless trimmed lamb, leg or chops
1 tablespoon olive oil
2 sprigs rosemary or 1 teaspoon dried rosemary
2 sprigs thyme or 1 teaspoon dried thyme
Salt and pepper
Wild Rice with Fresh Corn (page 200)

If your skewers are made of bamboo, soak them in water for about half an hour to prevent them from catching on fire over the grill.

Cut the lamb pieces 1-inch square and place the cubes between sheets of plastic wrap. With a meat tenderizer, pound out the lamb very thin. Weave the lamb onto the skewers. Rub the meat with olive oil and sprinkle with rosemary and thyme. Shortly before grilling it, season the meat with salt and pepper.

Over a medium-hot grill, or in a sauté pan over medium-high heat, cook the lamb skewers for approximately 1 minute on each side. Serve the brochettes with wild rice and corn.

Serves 4

GRILLED RACK OF LAMB *with*

SPICY BELL PEPPER JELLY

The rack of lamb at Vincent's has become one of our signature dishes.
Actually the preparation of the lamb is kept quite simple. We use the most tender
cuts of young rack of lamb, rub them with olive oil, season with salt and pepper,
then grill them over mesquite wood to the desired degree of doneness.
The lamb is served with a "burning" sprig of rosemary, which has a very
fragrant smell that wafts through the dining room. It is necessary that fresh rosemary
be dried by putting it in the oven for approximately 20 minutes at 325°F. Or you
can just leave it in the sun for a few days. Just before serving, light the sprig and
quickly blow it out. The scent will linger for several minutes. In fact, guests have
inquired whether the chefs were smoking something funny in the kitchen!
I developed the jelly to go with our grilled rack of lamb as an alternative to the
usual mint jelly. During a trip to Santa Fe shortly after our restaurant opened
in Phoenix, I tried some jalapeño *jelly in a little gourmet shop. I liked the prickly*
hot sensation on my palate, the spiciness of the peppers coupled with the
sweetness of the jelly. When I came back to the restaurant I began experimenting
and came up with our spicy bell pepper jelly, which gives you a hot and sweet taste
all in the same bite. It does for the lamb what barbecue sauce does for beef ribs.
We've also found that it is delicious with goat cheese nachos, *plain corn chips,*
or even over a soft cheese such as brie *served with crackers.*
It keeps well for quite a while in the refrigerator.

8 racks of lamb, each weighing between 12 and 14 ounces and trimmed of all fat
Salt and pepper
8 sprigs of dried rosemary
Spicy Bell Pepper Jelly (recipe follows)

*P*repare the bell pepper jelly first.

Season the lamb with salt and pepper. Grill the lamb (or sauté it if a grill is not available) over mesquite: 3 minutes per side for rare; 6 minutes per side for medium; and 9 to 10 minutes per side for well-done.

To serve, cut the lamb into chops and arrange on serving plates. Add a sprig of the dried rosemary. Set each sprig alight, blow out the flame at once, and serve the dish immediately (so that the essence of rosemary is fresh) with spicy bell pepper jelly.

Serves 8

SPICY BELL PEPPER JELLY

2 red bell peppers
2 yellow bell peppers
2 green bell peppers
8 red *serrano chiles*
2 cups sugar

Slice or julienne the peppers and *chiles,* but do not remove the seeds. Mix in the sugar and let the mixture sit overnight in the refrigerator. The following day, cook the mixture over low heat for between 10 and 15 minutes without adding any liquid. The peppers and *chiles* mixed with sugar will create their own liquid. Cool the jelly and serve at room temperature.

Makes 2 cups

Roasted Leg of Lamb *with*
Garlic & Jalapeños

The roasted jalapeños *inserted into the meat suffuse the lamb
with their flavor but do not overpower the flavor of the lamb itself.*

6 whole *jalapeño* peppers

1 leg of lamb, weighing between 6 and 8 pounds, trimmed of fat, bone intact

3 tablespoons olive oil

2 tablespoons pure *chile* powder

Salt and pepper

12 heads garlic, root ends cut off

1 sprig fresh thyme or ½ teaspoon dried thyme

1 sprig fresh rosemary or ½ teaspoon dried rosemary

1 cup water

¼ cup chicken glaze (page 265)

*P*reheat the oven to 400°F. Blister the *jalapeño* peppers in a hot oven or over a high flame. Once they are blackened, cut each pepper in half lengthwise, but do not peel it. Make 12 slits in the lamb and slide 1 half of a *jalapeño* into each slit. Brush the leg of lamb with 1 tablespoon of the olive oil. Dust the lamb with *chile* powder, salt, and pepper.

Sauté the lamb in the remaining 2 tablespoons of olive oil over medium-high heat or over a grill until the meat is lightly browned on all sides. Place the meat in a roasting pan and surround it with the garlic heads, thyme, and rosemary. Cook uncovered for approximately 45 minutes, turning the leg 3 to 4 times during the cooking period. After 45 minutes, remove the leg of lamb and the garlic heads and set them aside. Add the water and chicken glaze to the pan and bring the mixture to a boil. Cook for 2 to 3 minutes or until the liquid is reduced. Serve each portion of lamb with 1 head of garlic per person and top each serving with a tablespoon of cooking juices.

Serves 8 to 10

Pork

Americans eat a lot of pork, most of it as ham. The perception that pork must be *very* well cooked in order to be safe is still widespread. A beautiful loin of pork does not need to be roasted until it is gray and dry. Pork that is still a little pink is far juicier and tastier and, as long as the internal temperature is above 131°F (at which stage it is still much too rare for most tastes anyway), it will be perfectly safe. Pork takes very well to the grill and is enhanced by sweet flavors.

GRILLED PORK CHOPS *with* GARLIC

When grilling these chops, take them off the fire just before
you think they will be done; they will continue to cook while
they are set aside waiting for the garnish to be prepared.

8 cloves garlic
4 pork chops, each weighing about 8 ounces
1 tablespoon olive oil
Salt and pepper
Juice of 1 lemon, at room temperature
1 tablespoon chopped parsley

$\mathcal{P}$eel the garlic cloves, blanch them, and cut them in half.
Make 4 small cuts in each side of the pork chops and insert
half a garlic clove into each slit. Brush the chops with olive oil
and season them with salt and pepper. Grill the chops for between 6 and 7 minutes over a hot fire. When the chops are
cooked, set them aside briefly. Mix the lemon juice and
chopped parsley together. Serve the pork with the garlic still
inside, garnished with about ¾ teaspoon of the parsley mixture on top of each chop.

Serves 4

GRILLED PORK TENDERLOIN *with*
CASCABEL CHILE & HONEY GLAZE

Cascabel chiles are so lovely that it is almost a pity to grind them up to make this glaze. Dried, they are the size of large cherries, a dark, glossy mahogany-red brown. Inside, the dried seeds are loose and rattle when the chile *is shaken, hence the name, which means little bell.*

3 pork tenderloins, each weighing approximately 14 ounces
3 tablespoons olive oil
1 teaspoon salt
2 teaspoons coarse ground black pepper
Cascabel Chile and Honey Glaze (recipe follows)

*P*repare the *cascabel chile* and honey glaze (the *chiles* must soak for two hours before using).

Prepare a medium-hot grill and, while it is heating, rub the tenderloins with olive oil and season them with salt and pepper. Over a medium-hot grill cook the tenderloins for approximately 10 minutes, turning them frequently. (Or sauté them.) Brush the meat with the *cascabel chile* and honey glaze and cook it for an additional 2 minutes on each side. Remove the pork tenderloins from the grill and allow the meat to rest for 5 minutes before slicing it. On the bias, cut each tenderloin into slices, 6 per serving. Drizzle the remaining honey glaze over the sliced pork.

Serves 6

Cascabel Chile & Honey Glaze

4 dried *cascabel chiles* (if they are not available, substitute 2 *jalapeños*)
1 cup honey
½ cup chicken stock (page 264)
3 tablespoons tomato purée
1 teaspoon paprika
1 teaspoon ground cumin

Rehydrate the *cascabel chiles* by soaking them in warm water for about 2 hours before using them. Drain the *chiles* and place them with the honey, chicken stock, tomato purée, paprika, and cumin in a saucepan and simmer the mixture over medium heat for approximately 10 minutes. Remove from the heat and purée the mixture in a blender.

If *jalapeños* are used, roast them (page 266) and peel, seed, and dice them before simmering them with the rest of the ingredients.

Makes 1 ½ cups

Pork Skewers *with*

Cilantro & Jalapeño

The more pungent herbs, rosemary and sage, are customarily served with pork. The southwestern equivalent is this recipe, in which pork is partnered by the equally assertive cilantro and chile *peppers.*

4 wood skewers, about 8 inches long
1 pound pork loin
4 fresh *jalapeño* peppers
1 tablespoon olive oil
2 tablespoons chopped cilantro
2 tablespoons unsalted butter
1 tablespoon lemon juice

Soak the skewers in water to prevent their burning on the grill.

Cut the pork loin into 16 medium-sized cubes. Cut the *jalapeños* in quarters and remove the seeds. Alternate pieces of pork and *jalapeño* on the skewers: 4 cubes of pork and 4 pieces of *jalapeño* on each skewer. Brush the skewers with olive oil and grill them over medium heat for approximately 3 or 4 minutes on each side—a total of 6 or 8 minutes.

To make a sauce, melt the cilantro and butter together until the butter is foamy. Add the lemon juice. Serve the skewers with a little of the sauce around each.

Serves 4

Pork Roast *with* Onions & Apples

*Traditionally pork and apples are served together in Europe.
In this version, roast pork is treated according to my
southwestern style of cooking: The pungency and sweetness of
one ingredient, the onions, both contrasts with and complements
the tartness and sweetness of another, the apples.*

1 pork butt, weighing 5 pounds
Salt and pepper
½ cup olive oil
3 heads garlic, cut in half horizontally
1 branch thyme or 1 teaspoon dried thyme
1 branch rosemary or 1 teaspoon dried rosemary
5 large onions, peeled and sliced thinly
10 Red Delicious apples, cored and thinly sliced, but not peeled

*P*reheat the oven to 300°F.

Season the pork butt with salt and pepper to taste. Heat the
olive oil in a heavy ovenproof skillet. When the oil is hot,
place the pork butt in the skillet and brown it on all sides;
this will take approximately 2 minutes per side. Arrange the
garlic, thyme, and rosemary in the pan around the pork.
Roast the meat in the skillet, uncovered, for approximately 1
hour. Add the onions to the pan, arranging them to surround
the sides and cover the top of the pork. Continue to bake uncovered for approximately 1 hour longer. To ensure that the
meat cooks evenly, turn the pork every 15 minutes. After the
second hour, add the sliced apples and cook for an additional
30 minutes or until the apples are cooked and tender.

Serves 8 to 10

Veal

Veal is now much more appreciated in this country than it used to be, and I think that is because the quality of the veal itself has improved. No longer anemic and tasteless, good quality veal, though expensive, is one of the most flavorful and delicate of meats.

Grilled Veal Sweetbreads *with*
Red Wine & Thyme Sauce

*Veal sweetbreads are a delicacy not appreciated by everyone,
perhaps because they are very, very rich and have an odd texture,
but I adore them, and they make for a very special meal. Sweetbreads
from milk-fed veal are considered the best because of their creamy-smooth
texture and delicate flavor. They should be plump, firm, and white when purchased;
a redder or darker color would indicate an older animal. Sweetbreads are
highly perishable and should be used within a day. They should be soaked
in acidulated water for twenty-four hours before being cooked.*

2 pounds veal sweetbreads

4 quarts water

2 lemons, each sliced in half

4 bay leaves   5 cloves garlic

4 tablespoons salt

2 tablespoons black peppercorns

Olive oil, for cooking

Red Wine and Thyme Sauce (recipe follows)

Soak the sweetbreads, keeping them in the refrigerator, in acidulated water for 24 hours before cooking them. The water should be changed at least once every 8 hours.

To cook the sweetbreads, combine 4 quarts plain water with the lemon halves, bay leaves, garlic, salt, and black peppercorns; bring the mixture to a boil and add the sweetbreads. Cook for approximately 10 minutes, until the sweetbreads are firm but still slightly soft in the center. Transfer the drained sweetbreads to a bowl of ice water and allow them to cool.

Once they are cool, under running water peel the membrane away from the sweetbreads and discard it. Place the sweetbreads in between 2 pans, weight the top pan, and press the meat for at least 2 hours. Make the sauce.

When you are ready to serve, divide the sweetbreads into 6 portions, rub each with olive oil, and season with salt and pepper. Over a medium-hot grill, cook the sweetbreads for 3 or 4 minutes on each side. If a grill is not available, sauté them in olive oil.

Serve the sweetbreads with red wine and thyme sauce and, if you like, wild mushroom ragout (page 199).

Serves 6

RED WINE & THYME SAUCE

2 cups red wine
¼ cup fresh thyme leaves
¼ cup minced shallots
½ cup veal stock (page 266)
1 cup (2 sticks) unsalted butter, cut into cubes

Combine the red wine, thyme, and shallots and reduce over medium heat until the liquid is gone. Add the stock and reduce over very low heat until ¼ cup liquid remains. Slowly add the butter, keeping the heat low, until the butter has melted. Strain the sauce and keep it warm in a water bath until you are ready to serve it.

Makes 1¼ cups

ROASTED VEAL CHOPS *with* CHIPOTLE BEURRE BLANC

In this recipe a rack of veal is roasted in the oven and then cut into individual chops. At the restaurant we usually serve these chops with parsnip purée (page 190) as well as the chipotle beurre blanc, *which has an earthy, velvety taste and a beautiful burnt-orange color— both elements of what I consider southwestern cooking.*

1 tablespoon olive oil
1 rack of veal, weighing between 2 ½ and 3 pounds, trimmed
Salt and pepper
Chipotle *Beurre Blanc* (page 268)

*P*reheat the oven to 400°F. Heat the olive oil in a skillet and sauté the veal on high heat for between 3 and 4 minutes, giving it a nice brown color. Remove the meat from the skillet and season it with salt and pepper to taste.

Roast the veal in the preheated oven for approximately 30 minutes; it will be medium rare. While the veal is cooking, prepare the *chipotle beurre blanc*. Remove the meat from the oven and let it stand for 15 minutes before slicing the rack into 4 chops.

Serve the veal chops with the *chipotle beurre blanc*.

Serves 4

GRILLED VEAL LOIN *with*

CHIPOTLE PASTA &

FRIED SHALLOTS

I serve chipotle pasta with veal often because the spicy pasta goes nicely with the mild flavor of the veal. The fried shallots add some crunchiness and, because they are milder in taste than onions are, they don't overpower the pasta.

½ recipe Chipotle Pasta (page 96)
8 slices veal loin, each weighing 3 ounces
4 tablespoons olive oil
4 tablespoons chopped shallots
Salt and pepper
2 tablespoons butter or olive oil

*P*repare the pasta a day in advance and set the noodles aside to dry.

Brush the slices of veal loin with 1 tablespoon of the olive oil and grill the meat over high heat for 3 minutes on each side. Or sauté it over medium-high heat.

Heat the remaining 3 tablespoons of the olive oil in a skillet over high heat. When the oil is very hot, add the shallots and stir-fry them until they are golden brown. Season with salt and pepper to taste.

Cook the pasta in a large pot of boiling salted water for about 3 minutes, or until *al dente*. Drain, toss with butter or olive oil, and serve topped with the veal and garnished with the fried shallots.

Serves 4

Beef

Nothing is more American than a great slab of beef—even if the first cattle were brought over to the Southwest from Spain by Vásquez de Coronado in 1540. Americans do more with beef than any other people on earth and, I think, American beef is better than any other on earth—especially when it is raised on corn in the West.

The strong basic flavor of beef doesn't need much in the way of other ingredients to make it taste any better, and I like to serve it as simply as possible.

163

CHIMAYÓ CHILE BURGERS

*A few years ago there was a local contest in Scottsdale for the best hamburger,
and our name was submitted as an entrant. We're not exactly known
for serving burgers, so we had to come up with something in our style.
My chef did us proud with this recipe: an example of taking an old favorite
and hitching it up a few notches. Now we even occasionally put them on our
dining room menu. When first-timers bite into this burger and discover the
luscious melted cheese inside rather than on top, they break out in surprised smiles,
then shake their heads and wonder why no one's ever thought of this before.*

4 Anaheim (New Mexico) *chiles,* roasted (page 266)
3½ pounds ground beef ☙ Salt and pepper
2 teaspoons pure *chile* powder ☙ 2 tablespoons olive oil
2 cups shredded *jalapeño*-flavored Monterey Jack cheese
Bell Pepper and Pine Nut Brioche Buns (page 206)
Chipotle Mayonnaise (page 63)
Tomato, red onion, and avocado slices, for garnish

*P*repare the bell pepper and pine nut brioche buns and the
chipotle mayonnaise and set aside. Peel the roasted *chiles,* then
split them down the center, and remove the seeds.

Divide the ground beef into 16 portions and make patties.
Season each patty with salt, pepper, and *chile* powder, and
brush it with olive oil. Using 2 patties for each burger, place
half a peeled green *chile* and ¼ cup shredded cheese between
the patties and press them firmly together to seal in the "filling" completely.

Grill the burgers to the desired doneness. Serve the burgers in bell pepper and pine nut brioche buns, with *chipotle*
mayonnaise and garnished with slices of tomato, red onion,
and avocado.

Serves 8

GRILLED FILLET OF BEEF

*This recipe provides a slightly different twist to good old
meat and potatoes. If you don't like the strong flavor of thyme,
you can omit it from the recipe but it does add a nice aroma and
taste when used sparingly. If you cannot grill the meat outdoors,
it can be seared in a cast iron skillet or broiled.
With it we serve whipped potatoes and an onion compote
that adds a sweetness that I like with the beef and garlic.*

1 ½ pounds beef tenderloin, cut into 8 medallions, each weighing 3 ounces
1 tablespoon olive oil
1 teaspoon salt
1 ½ teaspoons coarsely ground black pepper
Whipped Potatoes (page 192)
Red Onion Compote (page 189)

If you are serving them, prepare the whipped potatoes and
the red onion compote first.

Rub the medallions of beef with olive oil, salt, and pepper.
Cook the beef over a hot grill (or sauté it on medium heat) for
approximately 2 minutes on each side, for medium rare; increase the cooking time according to taste. Serve at once with
whipped potatoes and red onion compote.

Serves 4

Grilled New York Steak *with* Roasted Green Chile & Corn Relish

Bon Appetit magazine published this recipe after its managing editor enjoyed it at our restaurant. As a result, the American Beef Council also chose it for an ad campaign of theirs. It's perfect for a good hearty meal when nothing else but a steak will do! Fried onions (page 188) make a particularly good accompaniment.

6 New York steaks, each weighing between 8 and 10 ounces
1 tablespoon olive oil
Salt and freshly ground black pepper
Roasted Green Chile and Corn Relish (recipe follows)
Fried Onions (page 188)

*P*repare the relish and the onions first and set them aside, keeping them warm.

Rub the steaks with olive oil and season them with salt and pepper. Cook the steaks on a hot grill or over medium-high heat in a sauté pan for approximately 4 minutes on each side; they will be medium rare. Arrange the steaks on a serving plate with fried onions and some of the green *chile* and corn relish.

Serves 6

Roasted Green Chile & Corn Relish

2 ears fresh corn or 1 cup frozen corn kernels, defrosted

1 teaspoon olive oil

Quarter of a red onion, finely diced

3 cloves garlic, finely minced

4 Anaheim (New Mexico green) *chiles,* roasted (page 266),
peeled, seeded, and diced, or substitute two 4-ounce cans diced green *chiles*

1 medium tomato, peeled, seeded, and diced

¼ cup chicken or veal stock (pages 264, 266)

1 bunch cilantro or 1 tablespoon dried parsley

Salt and pepper

Shuck the corn and blanch the ears in boiling water for 3 minutes. Allow the corn to cool and then cut the kernels off the cobs. Heat the olive oil in a medium pan and sauté the red onion and garlic until they are translucent. Add the diced green *chiles,* tomato, and corn and mix well. Add the stock and simmer the mixture for 5 minutes. Add the cilantro and season with salt and pepper. Set the relish aside, keeping it warm, while cooking the steak.

New York Steak *with*

Roquefort Sauce

*Funny thing about sirloin strips: The same superbly tender,
beefy cut is referred to either as a "New York" steak or a
"Kansas City" steak, depending on where you live. Whatever you
call them, they are my favorite cut, and if you like no-holds-barred
richness, this is a dish for you. The addition of a little port wine
to the Roquefort sauce makes a lot of sense; port is the
traditional accompaniment to blue-veined cheeses.*

2 tablespoons green peppercorns, rinsed
2 tablespoons oil
2 New York steaks, each weighing 8 ounces
1 medium garlic clove, minced
$\frac{1}{2}$ cup port
$\frac{1}{3}$ cup (about 3 ounces) Roquefort or other blue cheese, crumbled
$\frac{1}{3}$ cup heavy cream
2 teaspoons finely chopped parsley, for garnish

Crush the green peppercorns with a mortar and pestle and
set them aside. In a medium skillet large enough so that the
steaks will fit easily, heat the oil over medium-high heat. Sear
the steaks for about 4 minutes on the first side and 3 minutes
on the second; they will be medium rare. Transfer the meat to

a platter and cover to keep it warm. Pour any excess drippings out of the pan. Add the garlic, crushed green peppercorns, and port and boil the mixture over high heat until the liquid is reduced by half. Whisk in the Roquefort cheese and cream to thicken the sauce. Heat, still whisking, until the cheese melts. Pour some of the sauce on each serving plate and place a steak on top of the sauce. (The steak may be sliced for an attractive presentation.) Garnish with parsley and serve immediately.

Serves 2

TENDERLOIN OF BEEF

Now here is a classic French recipe that needs no alteration.

1 whole tenderloin of beef, weighing about 3 to 4 pounds, trimmed
2 tablespoons melted unsalted butter
2 tablespoons soy sauce
1 shallot, finely chopped
Roasted Shallots and Tarragon (page 195)

*P*reheat the oven to 425°F and, if you are serving them, prepare the roasted shallots first. While they are cooking, prepare the roast. Tuck the tail end of the tenderloin underneath so that the entire piece of meat is of the same thickness. Tie the meat tightly with string lengthwise and crosswise. Combine the butter, soy sauce, and chopped shallot and rub the mixture over the meat thoroughly.

Sear the meat in a pan on top of the stove until it has a nice, brown crust on all sides. Place the meat on a roasting rack so that it will cook evenly and roast it for between 15 and 20 minutes, or until a meat thermometer registers 130°F for rare, 140°F for medium rare, and 160°F for medium to well done.

When the beef is ready, remove it from the oven and let it rest for 10 minutes. Slice the roast and divide it evenly among the serving plates. Serve with roasted shallots and a little of the cream from the shallot pan as a sauce.

Serves 4

BEEF RIBEYE *with*

SPICY WATERCRESS SAUCE

*The ribeye is a fairly fatty, sometimes chewy, piece of meat preferred in
the West over sirloins and fillets. It is just as often used in French bistros
as the basis for the renowned* biftek *that is served with* pommes frites.
I wanted to spice up this cut of beef, and the jalapeños *pack a wallop.
You may want to tone it down according to your own taste.*

8 *jalapeño* peppers
1 tablespoon olive oil
2 cups fresh watercress leaves
1 cup chicken stock (page 264)
Salt and pepper
4 ribeye steaks, each weighing 8 ounces

Roast 4 of the *jalapeños* whole (page 266) and set them
aside, keeping them warm. Dice the 4 remaining *jalapeños*.
Heat the olive oil and sauté the watercress and diced *jalapeños*
for 2 minutes. Add the chicken stock and salt and pepper to
taste and bring the mixture to a boil. Purée the mixture in a
blender until the sauce is smooth. Set the sauce aside, keeping
it warm.

Grill the steaks over hot coals, or sauté them, for 4 or 5
minutes on each side; they will be medium rare.

To serve, put a ribeye steak on each plate, surround the
steak with watercress sauce, and top it with a roasted *jalapeño*
pepper as garnish. Serve immediately.

Serves 4

Beef & Anasazi Bean Chili

with Caciotta &

Frizzled Blue Corn Tortillas

*One day a good friend brought me some Anasazi beans,
named after the ancient cliff-dwelling Anasazi Indians of the Southwest.
I was not familiar with them and was intrigued by their red and
white color and spotted appearance. Thinking that they might make
a good chili, I first served them in Los Angeles at a Meals
on Wheels fundraiser for a thousand people.
Caciotta is a small, round Italian cheese. You might substitute
Monterey Jack or Cheddar in this recipe.*

1 cup diced raw bacon

1 red bell pepper, diced

1 medium red onion, diced

1 pound (2 cups) Anasazi beans, soaked overnight and drained

2 cups fresh, canned, or frozen corn kernels

1 sprig fresh rosemary or 1 teaspoon dried rosemary

4 heads roasted garlic (page 267)

8 cups water

2 tablespoons olive oil

1 pound beef tenderloin, trimmed and diced into ½-inch cubes

Salt and pepper

2 small, 6-inch blue corn tortillas

1 cup *caciotta* or Monterey Jack cheese

In a stock pot, sauté the diced bacon until the fat runs, add
the bell pepper and red onion and cook until the vegetables
are lightly browned. Add the beans, corn, rosemary, garlic,

water, and 1 tablespoon of the olive oil. Bring the mixture to a boil and simmer for approximately 30 minutes.

Season the beef tenderloin cubes with salt and pepper to taste and sauté them in the remaining tablespoon of olive oil. Add the cooked beef to the bean mixture. Continue to simmer the mixture for an additional 30 minutes.

To frizzle the tortillas, run the 2 blue corn tortillas through a pasta machine and deep-fry the resulting strips until they are crisp.

When you are ready to serve, sprinkle each portion of chili with *caciotta* cheese and frizzled blue tortillas.

Serves 8 to 10

Game

Game animals are grouped into two categories: large and small. The most common large game is venison, which usually refers to deer, although sometimes also to elk, moose, reindeer (caribou), or antelope. We generally use deer, but any of the game meat mentioned will work.

The venison in a commercial market will have been farm-raised and federally inspected. A wild animal *may* carry disease and parasites. As a result I serve only inspected, farm-raised game at the restaurant, unless a customer asks me to cook up his quarry just for him.

Several factors determine the quality of the meat: the age of the animal (younger animals are generally more tender); the season in which the animal was killed (fall is best because the animals have fattened up for winter and the cool weather is better for keeping the meat); and diet, which can, to some extent, affect the flavor of the meat.

The cut of the meat will usually determine its tenderness, just as it does with pork or beef. Wild game tends to be somewhat less tender than domesticated animals are. I've found that venison should be cooked slowly for maximum tenderness, but it is not always necessary to lard game if it is tender and succulent to begin with.

GRILLED QUAIL *with* JÍCAMA ♥

*Fresh, farm-raised quail is usually available
year-round through specialty butchers. Quail has a delicate
flavor and goes well with the texture of the jícama.
Often referred to as a Mexican potato, jícama has white crunchy flesh,
a sweet flavor, and is a good source of vitamin C and potassium.
If you are unable to find jícama, you can substitute
firm-fleshed fruit, such as apple or pear, in this recipe.*

2 medium *jícama*, peeled and julienned
¼ cup lemon juice
¼ cup plus 1 tablespoon olive oil
¼ cup diced mixed yellow, red, and green bell peppers
1 tablespoon chopped cilantro
1 tablespoon diced tomato
Salt and pepper
4 large quail, approximately 4 ounces each

Mix together the *jícama*, lemon juice, ¼ cup of the olive oil, the diced bell pepper, cilantro, and tomato. Add salt and pepper to taste.

Brush the quail with the remaining tablespoon of olive oil and grill or sauté them for 8 to 10 minutes on all sides.

To serve, divide the *jícama* mixture among 4 plates and set the quail, each cut into quarters, on top.

Serves 4

GRILLED SQUAB *with*

BORDELAISE SAUCE

A squab is a young, domesticated pigeon that has never flown and is very tender. It is usually available during the summer and in some places year round. You can also find them frozen. Birds should be plump and firm when purchased and should be stored in the same manner as chicken. The Bordelaise sauce complements it nicely.

6 whole, boned squab, weighing approximately 8 ounces each
2 tablespoons olive oil
12 whole dried bay leaves
Bordelaise Sauce (recipe follows)
Wild Rice with Fresh Corn (page 200)

*P*repare the sauce first and, while it is simmering, cook the squab.

Brush the squab with olive oil. Slide two bay leaves under the skin on the breast side of each bird. Grill the squab over hot mesquite for approximately 7 minutes on each side. Put the birds on a platter and let them sit, keeping them warm, for approximately 10 minutes. Save the juice, which will drain from the birds onto the platter; add it to the Bordelaise sauce, and finish off the sauce while the grilled squab are resting.

To serve, place each squab on a bed of wild rice and fresh corn and pour some of the sauce around the vegetables.

Serves 6

BORDELAISE SAUCE

1 bottle (750 ml; 3 cups) red Bordeaux wine
¼ cup chopped shallots
2 sprigs fresh thyme or 1 teaspoon dried thyme
2 sprigs fresh rosemary or 1 teaspoon dried rosemary
1 tablespoon coarsely ground black peppercorns
2 cups veal stock (page 266)
1 tablespoon chicken glaze (page 265)
Juice from the grilled squab
8 tablespoons (1 stick) unsalted butter, softened

Pour the wine into a skillet and add the shallots, thyme, rosemary, and peppercorns. Bring the mixture to a boil. Over low heat, reduce the liquid to approximately ½ cup. This will take about 20 minutes. Add the veal stock and chicken glaze. Simmer for approximately 15 minutes. Add the juice from the grilled squab and strain the sauce. Whisk in the butter until the mixture is smooth. Serve the sauce hot.

SAUTÉED VENISON LOIN *with*

RED WINE SAUCE

We serve this venison with a simple red wine sauce because you don't want a sauce that is going to compete with the rich flavor of the meat.

2 pounds trimmed venison loin

2 cups red wine

1 carrot, peeled and roughly chopped

2 stalks celery, washed and roughly chopped

Half a yellow onion, roughly chopped

1 head garlic, cut in half horizontally

2 whole bay leaves

2 sprigs fresh rosemary or 1 teaspoon dried rosemary

1 sprig fresh thyme or 1 teaspoon dried thyme

1 teaspoon black peppercorns

Salt and freshly ground black pepper

2 tablespoons olive oil

Blue Corn Pancakes (page 204)

Red Wine Sauce (recipe follows)

6 sprigs fresh rosemary, for garnish

*P*lace the trimmed venison loin in a deep pan and cover it with the red wine. Add the roughly chopped carrot, celery, onion, garlic, bay leaves, herbs, and peppercorns. Marinate the meat in the refrigerator for between 8 and 12 hours or overnight.

Drain the venison and reserve the marinade. Prepare the sauce and set it aside while cooking the venison.

When you are ready to cook, preheat the oven to 400°F and pat the meat dry. Cut the loin into 6 portions and season them with salt and black pepper on both sides.

Heat the olive oil on medium-high heat and sauté the venison for approximately 3 minutes on each side. Put the meat in a baking dish and place it in the oven for 5 minutes. Remove the venison from the oven and, keeping it warm, allow it to sit for 5 minutes. Cut each portion of venison into 5 or 6 slices. Arrange the slices on each serving plate with the blue corn pancakes. Pour some of the sauce over the meat and garnish each serving with a sprig of fresh rosemary.

Serves 6

RED WINE SAUCE

Reserved venison marinade
4 cups veal stock (page 266)
8 tablespoons (1 stick) unsalted butter, softened

In a saucepan, over medium-high heat, reduce the venison marinade by half; this will take between 20 and 30 minutes. Add the veal stock and reduce the liquid by half again. Remove the pan from the heat and whisk in the softened butter. Strain the sauce and keep it hot until you are ready to serve.

Makes 2 1/2 cups

RABBIT LEGS *with* TOMATOES & BASIL♥

Although many Americans feel a little squeamish about eating rabbit,
it is widely eaten in the West and all over Europe. I grew up eating
rabbit and I love the taste, so I hope to make some converts with this dish.

2 tablespoons olive oil
4 rabbit legs
Salt and pepper
4 large tomatoes, blanched, peeled, and quartered
1 cup chopped fresh basil leaves
1 cup chicken stock (page 264)

*H*eat the olive oil in a large sauté pan. Season the rabbit legs
with salt and pepper and brown them in the oil for approximately 5 minutes on all sides. Add the tomatoes and ½ cup of
the basil. Sauté for an additional 5 minutes. Add the chicken
stock and simmer for 15 minutes over low heat. Remove the
legs and slice them. Arrange the tomatoes on the serving
plates and the slices of rabbit over the tomatoes. Sprinkle the
remaining basil over the top.

Serves 4

VEGETABLES

We are so blessed in the West with such an incredible variety of fresh vegetables. They are raised locally in Arizona or come in from the other western states, particularly California. Many of them I was completely unfamiliar with when I arrived in Arizona, but I've learned not only to love them but also to understand many of them—including corn, *chiles,* and many wild mushrooms.

I like my vegetables relatively simple in order to maintain their essential flavors.

GRILLED CORN

*Grilling may be among the easiest ways to cook vegetables—
especially if you are already grilling the meat or fish
that the vegetable might accompany.*

4 ears corn, with husks
4 tablespoons butter
4 teaspoons pure Chimayó *chile* powder
Salt and pepper

Open the husks but do not peel them off. Remove the silk
from the corn and wash the ears. Brush each ear with 1 tablespoon of the butter and then sprinkle it with 1 teaspoon of the
chile powder. Add salt and pepper if desired. Wrap the corn
back in the husks and tie the ends with a strip torn off a
husk. Grill the corn over hot mesquite or charcoal for approximately 25 minutes, turning the ears every 5 to 10 minutes.
May be served hot or cold.

Serves 4

Eggplant &

Goat Cheese Timbales

At the restaurant we serve these small timbales alongside sautéed or grilled lamb chops (page 146). Your guests will think you spent much more time preparing them than you actually did. I got the idea while dining at the renowned restaurant Jamin in Paris where they offer a similar presentation made with thinly sliced zucchini and ratatouille. Ours is a Southwest version of their idea.

1 small eggplant
2 tablespoons olive oil ❧ Salt and pepper
1 tablespoon pure Chimayó *chile* powder
3 ounces mild goat cheese
1 large tomato, peeled and diced
1 tablespoon chopped basil

*P*reheat the oven to 300°F and lightly oil 4 2-ounce ramekins.

Slice the eggplant into 10 very thin slices and cut each slice in half. Brush the slices with olive oil, season them with salt, pepper, and Chimayó *chile* powder, and grill them over a hot grill or sauté them for 2 minutes on each side. Set the eggplant aside.

Mix the goat cheese, diced tomato, and chopped basil. Line the bottoms of 4 oiled ramekins with the slices of eggplant (4 in each), making sure that you have some on the sides. Fill each ramekin with the goat cheese mixture and cover each cup with slices of eggplant. Bake for 20 minutes. Turn out onto serving plates and serve hot.

Serves 4

GARLIC PURÉE

We make purées a lot at the restaurant and offer them as accompaniments to meat and poultry in place of the usual potatoes or rice. As well as being served alone, purées can be combined: a parsnip purée mixed with mashed potatoes or a garlic purée are excellent.

2 pounds garlic (about 16 medium heads)
1 cup heavy cream
1 tablespoon unsalted butter
Salt and pepper

*P*eel the garlic and blanch the cloves by placing them in cold water and bringing the water to a boil. Drain the cloves and repeat the blanching procedure another 4 times. Combine the blanched garlic and the cream and simmer for approximately 5 minutes. Add the butter and purée the garlic mixture in a food processor. Add salt and pepper to taste and serve hot.

Serves 4

LEEK FLANS

*Flan, as a form of caramel custard, is by far the most popular dessert
in Mexico and Spain. Mine are different, more in the French style,
which can be either savory or sweet. They also make a great starter.
When purchasing leeks, look at the center of the leaves to
make sure the flower stalk isn't tough and hasn't started to form
a bulb at the bottom, which would indicate an older leek.
Younger, fresher leeks are for the most part straight.*

8 ounces green leeks
4 eggs, beaten
1 ½ cups heavy cream
Salt, pepper, and nutmeg to taste

*P*reheat the oven to 300°F and butter 8 individual, 2-ounce
ramekins.

Trim the roots and ends of the leaves and chop up the leeks.
Blanch them for 5 minutes. Drain the leeks and purée them in
a blender or food processor. Add eggs, the cream, and seasonings. Pour the mixture into the prepared ramekins and
bake the flans for 30 minutes. They are done when a toothpick inserted in the middle comes out clean. Serve hot.

Serves 8

GRILLED NOPALES

*Living in Arizona, we find fresh nopales (the so-called leaves,
or paddles, of the Opuntia or prickly pear cactus) fairly easy to obtain.
In some Hispanic markets they are available already
cleaned and also bottled or canned. As long as they are
not discolored at all, prepared nopales are quite acceptable.
To clean fresh nopales, grip the cactus with a pair of tongs and,
using a sharp knife, remove the thorns by carefully scraping off
the small bumps on the outside but do not peel away the outer layer
of green entirely. When the paddles are smooth they are ready to
be cooked. Boil them in salted water for between 5 and 10 minutes,
until they are tender. Do not overcook them or they will lose their
appealing crunchy texture and turn limp. Add the tops of some
scallions or green onions to the salted, boiling water; these seem
to help extract some of the slimy stickiness.*

4 medium-sized *nopales*
2 tablespoons olive oil
Salt and pepper

Clean the *nopales,* following the directions above. Do not
boil them but, instead, partially cook them in salted, boiling
water for about 5 minutes. Then immerse them in ice-cold
water for 5 minutes and pat them dry. Brush them with olive
oil and season with salt and pepper. Grill the *nopales* over a
hot fire for approximately 3 or 4 minutes on each side. Serve
warm.

Serves 4

FRIED ONIONS

*We serve these onions with New York steak (page 166), but they would
be suitable accompaniments to almost any dish that takes kindly to onions.*

1 cup flour
3 medium yellow onions, peeled and sliced very thin
Oil, for frying
Salt and freshly ground black pepper
Cayenne pepper

Flour the onions lightly and shake them in a sieve to remove
any excess flour. Heat the oil to a temperature of about 370°F
and deep-fry the onions in batches for 3 or 4 minutes, until
they are golden brown. Drain the onions and set them aside,
briefly, on paper towels. Season with salt, pepper, and cayenne and serve as soon as possible.

Serves 6

RED ONION COMPOTE

*Red onions seem to be particularly enhanced by
the combination of sweet and sour flavorings.*

2 red onions, peeled and cut into ½-inch dice
1 tablespoon unsalted butter
2 tablespoons sugar
¼ cup sherry vinegar
⅛ teaspoon salt
⅛ teaspoon freshly ground black pepper

Sauté the onions in the butter over medium-high heat for 5 minutes. Add the sugar and cook for 2 minutes, until the onions are lightly caramelized. Add the vinegar, salt, and pepper and cook for an additional 5 minutes over low heat.

Serve the compote warm.

Serves 4

Parsnip Purée

I love parsnips, a root similar to carrots or potatoes,
but far more flavorful and adaptable to new recipes.
(They are excellent when fried as chips.)
We serve parsnips under veal chops (page 161)
and top them with chipotle beurre blanc.

2 pounds fresh parsnips, peeled and cut into rough chunks
1 cup heavy cream
1 tablespoon unsalted butter
Salt and pepper

Steam the parsnips for 30 minutes. Heat the cream until it is hot but do not boil it. Purée the parsnips with the hot cream in a food processor. Add the butter and salt and pepper to taste. Serve hot.

Serves 4

GRILLED NEW POTATOES ♥

Another recipe to augment your repertoire of grilled vegetables.
Depending on what you are serving these with,
you might like to vary the flavoring herbs.

8 small new potatoes, red if possible
1 tablespoon olive oil
1 tablespoon dried thyme
1 tablespoon dried rosemary
Salt and pepper

Wash the potatoes, but do not peel them. Cut them in half. Blanch them in boiling salted water for 5 minutes and drain them. Brush the potatoes with olive oil and arrange them on small skewers. Grill the potatoes over high heat for 10 minutes on each side. Sprinkle with salt and pepper, thyme, and rosemary and serve hot.

Serves 4

WHIPPED POTATOES

People always comment on our whipped, or mashed, potatoes and how delicious they are. If you don't like the strong flavor of thyme, you can omit it from the recipe; I think it adds a nice aroma and taste when used sparingly and it goes particularly well with our grilled fillet of beef (page 165).

4 medium baking potatoes, peeled and quartered
12 cloves garlic, peeled
8 tablespoons (1 stick) unsalted butter
½ cup low-fat (2%) milk
1 teaspoon fresh thyme leaves
½ teaspoon salt
¼ teaspoon black pepper

Place the potatoes in a saucepan and cover with lightly salted water. Add the garlic cloves and boil over medium-high heat for approximately 30 minutes or until the vegetables are tender. Drain the potatoes and garlic and whip them. Fold in the butter, milk, and thyme and season with salt and pepper.

Serves 4

Potato Galettes

In France a galette *is generally made with pastry dough; I thought it would be fun to try one made with potatoes. They work well with many things, including smoked salmon or, in place of* blinis, *even caviar.*

1 cup cooked, mashed potato
¼ cup olive oil plus extra for frying
¼ cup chopped cilantro
1 tablespoon medium-hot, pure Chimayó *chile* powder
or regular *chile* powder
Salt and pepper

Mix the potato, ¼ cup of the oil, cilantro, and *chile* powder. Season to taste with salt and pepper. Shape the mixture into 16 small cakes. To cook the *galettes,* sauté them in olive oil over medium-high heat for approximately 1 or 2 minutes on each side, or until the potato cakes are golden brown on each side.

Makes 16 small galettes; *serves 4*

GRATIN DAUPHINOIS

However aristocratic this dish sounds (a dauphin is the eldest son of the French king), it's actually a simple, easy dish everyone can enjoy without much fuss. You can enrich it as much as you want with butter and cream or cut back and use just enough to give it flavor.

1 clove garlic
4 medium baking potatoes, peeled and sliced $1/10$ inch thick
1 cup heavy cream
2 teaspoons salt
2 teaspoons ground white pepper
$1/2$ cup grated Gruyère cheese (optional)

Preheat the oven to 375°F.

Crush the garlic and spread it on the bottom of a 8 by 8 by 1 $1/2$-inch baking pan. Layer the sliced potatoes with the cream in the pan, seasoning to taste with salt and pepper. Bake in the preheated oven for approximately 40 minutes or until the gratin is golden brown on top. If you wish, sprinkle grated Gruyère cheese on top of the baked potatoes and brown the cheese under the broiler.

Serves 4

Roasted Shallots & Tarragon

Tarragon is one of my favorite herbs and is used frequently in French cooking. This recipe has essentially the same flavoring as the classic béarnaise sauce. We serve these shallots with tenderloin of beef (page 170) and they cook at the same time.

16 large shallots
1 tablespoon butter, in small pieces
½ cup heavy cream
2 tablespoons Madeira or red wine
1 ½ teaspoons chopped fresh tarragon or ½ teaspoon dried tarragon
¼ teaspoon salt
Pinch of finely ground black pepper

Preheat the oven to 425°F.

Peel the shallots and cut part of the root end off, leaving enough of the root so that the layers of the shallot will hold together. Immerse the shallots in boiling water for 2 minutes and drain them thoroughly. Place the shallots in a small shallow baking dish and dot with the butter. Roast the shallots, uncovered, for 10 minutes. Mix the cream with the Madeira, tarragon, salt, and pepper and pour the mixture over the shallots. Return the shallots to the oven and continue to roast them for an additional 30 or 35 minutes, uncovered. Toward the end, watch the dish carefully: If the cream sauce separates, whisk in a little water and additional cream.

Serves 4

SWEET POTATO PURÉE

Sweet potatoes go so well with poultry that we would do well to think of serving them between times and not only at Thanksgiving.

2 pounds sweet potatoes
¼ cup butter
¼ cup heavy cream, heated
Salt and pepper

*P*eel the sweet potatoes, cut them into quarters, and boil them in salted water for 30 minutes or until they are tender. Drain and purée potatoes and then sieve the purée. Add the butter and hot cream and season to taste with salt and pepper.

Serves 4

RATATOUILLE

I grew up in various places around the Mediterranean. Ratatouilles *combining the most frequently used vegetables, herbs, and seasonings of Provence, in particular, but the entire region in general, in one hearty dish, are almost a summary of Mediterranean cooking. My mother made it regularly (and still does) and this is her recipe.* Ratatouille *can be served either hot or cold, and it goes with dozens of dishes such as grilled fillet of beef (page 170), sautéed venison loin (page 178), and grilled pork chops (page 153).*

¼ cup olive oil
1 red onion, peeled and diced
1 red bell pepper, cored and diced
1 yellow bell pepper, cored and diced
1 large eggplant, diced with skin still on
2 medium zucchini, diced with skin still on
1 whole tomato, diced with skin still on
4 cloves garlic, peeled and minced
2 teaspoons chopped fresh thyme leaves
2 tablespoons chopped fresh basil leaves
Salt and pepper

*P*reheat the oven to 400°F.

In a large ovenproof skillet or roasting pan, heat the olive oil over medium-high heat. Sauté the onion for 3 or 4 minutes, until it is translucent. Add the bell peppers and sauté for an additional 3 or 4 minutes, until they are tender. Add the eggplant and zucchini and sauté for an additional 3 or 4 minutes. Add the tomato, garlic, thyme, and basil. Season to taste with salt and black pepper.

Serves 4

SPINACH SOUFFLÉS

These light soufflés are delicious served at lunch or as a side dish.

2 teaspoons butter
2 teaspoons flour
⅓ cup milk
2 ½ to 3 cups blanched and chopped spinach
Salt and pepper
1 tablespoon lemon juice
2 egg whites

*P*reheat the oven to 400°F. Butter and flour 4 individual, 2-ounce ramekins.

Melt the butter over medium heat. Add the flour and mix to make a *roux*. Cook the *roux* for approximately 2 minutes. Add the milk and cook for approximately 1 minute more. Add the spinach, salt and pepper, and 2 teaspoons of the lemon juice. Keep the spinach mixture warm.

In a mixing bowl, beat the egg whites until they are stiff. Add a dash of salt and a few drops of lemon juice. Gently fold the egg white into the spinach mixture. Pour the mixture into individual ramekins and bake them for approximately 10 minutes, or until lightly browned on top. Serve hot.

Serves 4

WILD MUSHROOM RAGOUT

*A ragout generally has meat, fish, or poultry as its principal ingredient,
but the basic meaning of the name is a reference to the preparation
method: a stew. Any combination of mushrooms can be used.
At the restaurant, this ragout often accompanies sweetbreads
(page 159) or is served by itself in a fried potato nest.*

1 pound oyster mushrooms
1 teaspoon olive oil
1 teaspoon unsalted butter
½ teaspoon chopped garlic
1 teaspoon chopped shallots
1 tablespoon brandy
1 tablespoon veal glaze (optional)
¼ cup heavy cream
1 teaspoon fresh thyme leaves

Wash the mushrooms in cold water and pat them dry. Heat
the olive oil in a sauté pan over medium-high heat. Add the
mushrooms and cook them for approximately 4 minutes, stirring often. Add the butter, garlic, and shallots and cook for an
additional 3 minutes, continuing to lightly stir.

Add brandy, the veal glaze if you have it, and cream. Simmer the mixture for 5 minutes. Remove the mushrooms from
the heat and add the fresh thyme.

Serves 6

WILD RICE *with* FRESH CORN ♥

My wife loves this combination of wild rice and white rice with
fresh corn. The dish actually started by accident when we made
too much wild rice for another dish, so I ended up putting the rest
with some white rice. Leevon was at the restaurant that evening and
commented on how great it tasted. With the addition of a few
herbs and spices, the combination evolved into this recipe, which
goes particularly well with brochettes of lamb (page 147).

½ cup wild rice
4 cups chicken stock (page 264)
¼ cup long-grain white rice
½ cup fresh or frozen corn kernels, steamed
1 teaspoon olive oil
1 tablespoon peeled, seeded, and diced tomato
2 teaspoons salt
1 teaspoon ground black pepper
1 tablespoon chopped fresh parsley

*P*ut the wild rice in a pan with 3 cups of the chicken stock.
Bring the mixture to a boil, cover the pan, and simmer until
the liquid is absorbed; this will take about 45 minutes. In another pan, put the white rice and the remaining cup of chicken
stock and cook it following the same procedure; it will take
about 20 minutes. When they are cooked, combine the 2
kinds of rice and add the corn, olive oil, and tomato. Season
with salt and pepper, add the parsley, and serve hot.

Serves 4

BREADS

We make all our own breads and rolls at Vincent's, something very few restaurants in France would undertake because there they have access to wonderful bakeries on every corner.

Blue Corn Muffins

What a beautiful muffin this is! At the restaurant our presentation is quite spectacular because we bake them right in the corn husk. If you serve them in the husk, be sure to warn your guests not to eat the husks. If you don't have blue cornmeal available, you may substitute yellow or white for the muffins.

1 cup all-purpose flour ❧ 1 cup blue cornmeal
1 tablespoon baking powder
¾ cup grated *jalapeño*-flavored Cheddar cheese
¼ cup melted butter ❧ 2 tablespoons honey
2 eggs, beaten ❧ 1 cup milk
½ cup green *chile*, roasted (page 266), peeled, seeded, and diced
or ½ cup canned green *chile*, diced
¼ cup grated white cheese
12 dried corn husks (optional)

*P*reheat the oven to 350°F and lightly grease twelve 2-inch muffin cups.

Combine the flour, cornmeal, baking powder, and *jalapeño* cheese in a mixing bowl. In separate bowl, mix the butter, honey, eggs, milk, and green *chile* and add the mixture slowly to the dry ingredients. Stir only until just combined.

Pour the batter into the muffin cups, filling them three-quarters full. Sprinkle each muffin lightly with some of the white cheese. Bake the muffins for between 20 and 25 minutes, or until they are golden brown.

You may bake the muffins in corn husks. Tear each husk into 4 equal strips, laying the strips in a crisscross manner to line each muffin cup (the husks will protrude slightly above the cups). Fill the husks with batter and bake as directed.

Makes 12 small (2-inch) muffins

BLUE CORN PANCAKES

In my version of the pancake, I use southwestern blue cornmeal,
which alters the texture a bit but makes for a lot more flavor and color.

4 eggs
1 cup flour
¼ cup blue cornmeal
½ cup milk
½ cup heavy cream
1 tablespoon chopped red bell pepper
1 tablespoon chopped green bell pepper
1 tablespoon chopped yellow bell pepper
½ cup fresh, cooked corn kernels (from 1 ear of corn)
2 tablespoons chopped cilantro or 1 tablespoon dried parsley
½ teaspoon sugar
Salt and pepper

Place the eggs, flour, and cornmeal in a mixing bowl and mix until smooth. Add the milk and cream and mix well. Fold in the bell peppers, corn, cilantro, and sugar. Season to taste with salt and pepper.

Place 4 tablespoons of the batter on a hot griddle or in a nonstick pan and cook the pancakes for approximately 1 minute on each side.

Makes 16 pancakes

OLIVE ROLLS

I decided to make olive rolls after enjoying the terrific olive oil bread Wolfgang Puck makes at Spago. You'll also find fresh olive bread throughout the south of France, so these rolls always remind me of Europe. Our rolls are smaller and not as crusty, but they go very fast as soon as they're put down on the plate, hot from the oven.

6¾ cups sifted flour
2 tablespoons salt
2 tablespoons sugar
¾ cup chopped black olives
2⅓ cups water
⅓ cup plus 1 tablespoon olive oil
4 tablespoons (4 envelopes) active dry yeast

Mix the flour, salt, sugar, and olives in a food processor for a few seconds. Add the water, olive oil, and yeast and process until the mixture forms a small ball. (In this recipe, the yeast is *not* dissolved in water before being added to the flour mixture.) Let dough rise, covered and in a warm place, for approximately 1 hour. After the dough has tripled in size, punch it down and form it into 24 small balls, each about 1 inch in diameter.

Dust the tops of the rolls lightly with flour and make a criss-cross pattern on the top of each one with the tines of a fork. Let the rolls rise until they have doubled in size, about 1 hour. Preheat the oven to 350°F and bake the rolls for approximately 20 minutes or until they are golden brown.

Makes 24 rolls

BELL PEPPER &

PINE NUT BRIOCHE BUNS

These buns are designed to go with our award-winning burgers,
but you can just eat them on their own,
toasted for breakfast, or as a sandwich bun.

3 cups sifted flour

½ cup sugar

1 teaspoon salt

2 tablespoons (2 envelopes) active dry yeast

¼ cup warm water

6 whole eggs, slightly beaten

1½ cups (3 sticks) butter, softened

¼ cup toasted, chopped pine nuts

½ cup chopped bell peppers, red, yellow, or green or a combination

1 egg, beaten

In a mixing bowl, combine the flour, sugar, and salt. In a separate bowl, dissolve the yeast in the warm water and add the 6 eggs. Add the yeast mixture to the flour mixture and mix for between 8 and 10 minutes. Slowly add the butter and mix for 5 minutes. Fold in the pine nuts and peppers.

Set the dough aside, covered and in a warm place, until it has doubled; this will take about 2 hours. Punch the dough down and divide it into about 15 pieces. Form the pieces into gently rounded rolls. Let the rolls rise for about 30 minutes.

Preheat the oven to 375°F. Brush the tops with egg and bake for 15 minutes until the buns are golden brown.

Makes 14 to 16 buns

DESSERTS & DRINKS

Desserts

A lot of people say that they swear off desserts at the end of a meal, but we certainly haven't found that to be true at Vincent's. I like to think it's because we serve desserts that they won't find anywhere else and that ours are irresistible.

In every case I have applied the formal techniques of grand French pastrymaking to the wonderful ingredients I have found in this country. No one in France has ever had the temerity to combine orange with *jalapeño* peppers, but I believe this to be a good example of taking an odd idea and then using time-honored techniques to make it into something you wonder why no one ever thought of before.

Putting pumpkin and chocolate into a brownie may seem a little strange at first, but the combination works beautifully. Likewise, when people first taste my prickly pear sorbet, they are amazed at how good and refreshing it is.

Chefs are always playful when it comes to dessert, and people are a little bit more adventurous about trying them. So here are some fine traditional desserts along with some new concepts I've already seen being copied by my colleagues around America—though perhaps not just yet back in France.

FRUIT SALAD *with* AMARETTO CREAM SAUCE

The sauce turns an ordinary fruit salad into something special. This is a great dessert for brunch and works well for small groups or large ones. Only in summer can you use every fruit listed in the ingredients, but the salad can be made at any time of the year with whatever fruit is available at the time. The important point is to have as wide a variety of fruit as possible.

¼ pint raspberries ❧ ¼ pint blueberries
¼ pint strawberries, washed and cut in half
¼ cup orange segments, diced
¼ cup grapefruit segments, diced
¼ cup diced Granny Smith apple
¼ cup green grapes, preferably seedless
¼ cup diced peach ❧ ¼ cup diced apricot
¼ cup lemon juice
¼ cup plus 2 tablespoons sugar
1 tablespoon chopped mint ❧ ¼ cup heavy cream
2 egg yolks ❧ ¼ cup amaretto liqueur

Mix together all the fruit, the lemon juice, ¼ cup of the sugar, and the mint. Cover and refrigerate the salad overnight.

The following day, bring the cream to a boil and set the pan aside to cool slightly. Whisk the egg yolks and remaining 2 tablespoons sugar together. When the cream has cooled down sufficiently so that the eggs will not become scrambled, whisk in the egg and sugar mixture. Strain the sauce and stir in the liqueur. Serve the sauce in a small pitcher to pour over individual salad servings.

Serves 4

Fresh Fruit Salad *with*

Grapefruit Sorbet♥

Fresh fruit salad might seem to be so basic that most people know how to do it. We add a touch of sweet vermouth to this recipe to give it a little extra flavor. The presentation, in the center of the pineapple rings, is also interesting. An easy way to make the pineapple rings is to slice the pineapple and then use a doughnut cutter.

1 whole pineapple

1 orange

4 kiwifruit

2 Granny Smith apples

8 large strawberries

2 bananas

1 pint raspberries

2 tablespoons sugar

2 tablespoons white sweet vermouth

1 tablespoon lemon juice

8 sprigs fresh mint

Grapefruit Sorbet (page 251)

Slice the unpeeled pineapple into 8 rings, each approximately ½ inch thick. Carefully cut the fruit out of each slice, leaving the ring of peel intact so that the salad may be served in it. Set the pineapple skin rings aside. Remove and discard the core from each slice and dice the pineapple flesh. Peel the orange and divide it into segments. Peel the kiwi and cut each into 4 slices. Peel, core, and slice the apples. Wash and hull the strawberries, leaving them whole. Peel and slice the bananas. Mix all the fruit in a large bowl, adding the raspberries, sugar, sweet vermouth, and lemon juice. Let the salad marinate for approximately 1 hour in the refrigerator. Arrange the fruit in the center of the hollowed-out pineapple rings and garnish each serving with mint sprigs. Serve with a scoop of grape-fruit sorbet if desired.

Serves 8

APPLE SOUP♥

This soup is very light. It can be used to start a meal,
a light luncheon, for instance, and is also very good as a
light dessert served with a plain cake or cookies.

½ pound Red Delicious apples, sliced and cored, but not peeled
½ pound Granny Smith apples, sliced and cored, but not peeled
1 teaspoon ground cinnamon
2 cups orange juice
½ cup honey
Mint leaves, for garnish (optional)

Combine the sliced apples, cinnamon, orange juice, and honey in a saucepan and simmer the mixture for approximately 20 minutes. Purée in a blender, being careful to leave some chunks in the mixture.

The soup may be served hot or chilled and garnished with mint leaf if desired.

NOTE: This recipe is included with permission from the Growers of Washington State Apples, for whom it was originally developed.

Serves 4

Apples Baked in Parchment ♥

*Of course everyone has tried a baked apple, and they are usually good.
This recipe is a little different because the orange zest and vanilla bean that we
add give it extra complexity. (Remember that, when you remove the zest from
the orange, be careful to get only the colored part of the orange and not the white
pith, which has a bitter taste.) I particularly like McIntosh or Granny Smith apples
for baking, but Red Delicious will work also. Baking the apples in parchment
keeps the fruit from drying out and makes for easy cleanup.*

4 McIntosh or Granny Smith apples ❧ ¼ cup sugar
4 tablespoons orange zest ❧ 4 vanilla beans

Preheat the oven to 350°F. Cut apples in half horizontally
and remove seeds with a melon baller. Place ½ tablespoon of
the sugar into the cavity of each half apple and caramelize it:
A hand-held propane blow torch works best; just flame the
sugar until it turns to caramel (or, place the apples under a
preheated broiler for 1 or 2 minutes). Sprinkle orange zest on
top of the caramelized sugar.

For each serving, place two apple halves on a 12 by 10-inch
piece of parchment paper. Add 1 vanilla bean, which has been
slit to release the seeds (do not scrape out seeds). Fold in the
sides and close the top of the parchment paper, securing with
a toothpick if necessary. Bake the apples for approximately 20
or 25 minutes. Open the packages (but do not unwrap the apples entirely) and remove the vanilla beans. Serve hot.

NOTE: This recipe is included with permission from the
Growers of Washington State Apples, for whom it was developed.

Serves 4

213

DESSERTS & DRINKS

Pears Poached in Red Wine♥

Pears in syrupy red wine is a classic match of deep flavors. But like many classic recipes, it is quite high in calories. I was invited to make a very festive-looking holiday dessert on a local television program with the proviso that I keep the calorie count low. If you don't care about the calories, by all means serve this with whipped cream.

6 medium-sized fresh Anjou or Bosc pears (or your favorite variety)
1 small orange
6 whole cloves
4 cups dry red wine
1 cup plus 2 tablespoons sugar
Half a stick cinnamon

With a potato peeler, remove about half of the peel from the pears, leaving vertical strips of peel intact and giving the fruit a striped appearance. Stud the unpeeled orange with the cloves. Combine the wine, sugar, cinnamon stick, and orange in a stock pot. Bring the mixture to a boil and add the pears. Lower the heat to a simmer and cook the pears for approximately 30 minutes or until they are tender. Cool the mixture and chill pears in the cooking liquid.

To serve, put 1 whole pear on each serving plate with 1 or 2 tablespoons of the wine sauce around each pear.

Serves 6

FROZEN BLACKBERRY SOUFFLÉS

*I like frozen soufflés because they can be made in advance and
kept in the freezer. This recipe may be used with virtually any fruit,
using the same proportions, that is, ½ cup of fruit purée.
The liqueur may be omitted if desired. At the restaurant, we serve
them with a simple blackberry purée on the plate for color.
These soufflés need to be frozen overnight.*

1 cup heavy cream
1 pint fresh blackberries
1 ½ tablespoons blackberry brandy (optional)
1 ½ tablespoons *crème de cassis* (optional)
4 egg whites
½ cup sugar
Fresh blackberries for garnish

Prepare six 6-ounce ramekins by adding to each a strip of
waxed paper to form a collar secured by a rubber band. The
ramekins should then be about 3 inches deep.

Beat the cream until it is stiff. Purée the blackberries in a
food processor or blender and then pass the purée through a
sieve to remove the seeds. Add the blackberry brandy and
crème de cassis. Fold the berry mixture into the whipped
cream. Beat the egg whites until they are stiff. Slowly add the
sugar and continue to beat well until the mixture is smooth
and glossy. Fold the egg whites into the blackberry cream.
Spoon the soufflé mixture into the ramekins to the top of the
collars; smooth and freeze overnight.

To serve, remove the collars and garnish the tops of the
soufflés with fresh blackberries.

Serves 6

Grand Marnier Soufflé *with*

Orange Sauce

This soufflé is delicious and well worth the effort. You can use the same basic recipe and substitute another liqueur. Grand Marnier is my own favorite because it goes so well with the orange sauce, which should be made with fresh oranges and lemons if possible.

¼ cup plus 1 tablespoon sugar
5 eggs, separated
1 tablespoon Grand Marnier liqueur
1 teaspoon butter
Orange Sauce (recipe follows)

Prepare the sauce first and set it aside; it is served cold. Then preheat the oven to 425°F. Butter a soufflé dish and sprinkle it with 1 tablespoon of the sugar.

Using an electric mixer, beat the egg yolks, ¼ cup of the sugar, and liqueur together in a small mixing bowl until they are creamy and very thick. Using an electric mixer or wire whisk, beat the egg whites in a large mixing bowl until they form soft peaks. Fold the yolk mixture into the egg whites. Pour the soufflé mixture into the prepared dish and bake for between 8 and 12 minutes, or until it has doubled in height. Serve immediately, accompanied by orange sauce.

Serves 2 or 3

Orange Sauce

2 oranges
1 lemon
¼ cup heavy cream
3 tablespoons sugar

Zest the oranges and the lemon and place the zest in a medium saucepan. Squeeze the juice from both fruits and strain it into the saucepan with the zest.

Whip the cream in a bowl until it forms soft peaks but is not stiff. Bring the orange and lemon juice mixture to a boil; add the sugar, and stir until it has dissolved. Reduce the heat to medium and gently blend in the whipped cream. Continue to cook until the liquid has been reduced to one-third of its original volume. Set the sauce aside to cool.

CRÈME BRÛLÉE IN

"SWEET TACO SHELLS"

Our crème brûlée, *which is actually an English, not a French,
sweet, is by far our most popular dessert. I came up with the idea
of serving it in "taco" shells after it occurred to me that classic
French* tuiles *(tile-shaped cookies) would be perfect for holding
the custard and giving the dish an extra dimension.
In our kitchen we brown the sugar topping in an instant with a
hand-held blow torch, the kind you can find at most hardware stores.
But be very, very careful about using such a utensil at home.
If you don't have a torch, you may pour a light brown caramel sauce
over the custard and let it set until it forms a crackling crisp topping.*

Crème Brûlée
1 ⅓ cups heavy cream
⅔ cup sugar
1 vanilla bean
10 egg yolks
1 ⅔ to 4 pints (depending on the type) fruit:
strawberries, raspberries, blueberries, or peeled and diced kiwifruit

"Sweet Taco Shell"
½ cup (1 stick) butter
1 cup powdered sugar
4 egg whites
¾ cup flour

*P*repare the custard the night before it is to be served. Mix
the cream, sugar, and vanilla bean and bring the mixture to a
boil. With a whisk, beat the egg yolks and pour them gradually into the hot cream mixture, cooking the custard for

approximately 10 minutes over low heat. *Do not boil the mixture or the egg yolks will become scrambled.* When the mixture is thick, pour it into a stainless-steel bowl. Set the bowl into a larger bowl that has been filled with ice water to stop the custard from cooking. When the custard has cooled, cover the bowl with plastic wrap and refrigerate overnight.

Preheat the oven to 400°F, grease 2 baking sheets, and mark out 4 circles, each 3 inches across, on each sheet. Set out 8 drinking glasses, about 3 inches in diameter, turned upside down to be used as molds for the "shells."

In a mixing bowl combine the butter and sugar and beat until creamy. Slowly add the egg whites and then the flour. Place spoonfuls of the batter on the baking sheets in the center of each circle and spread the batter out thinly and evenly to fill the circle. Bake the cookies for approximately 7 or 8 minutes, or until they are golden brown.

Remove the baking sheets from the oven and, while the cookies are still warm, drape them over the drinking glasses. As they cool, the cookies will stiffen and will be used as the "taco shells."

To assemble the dessert, fill the bottom of the shells with fruit and, having removed the vanilla bean, spoon custard on top. Sprinkle the top of the custard with sugar and caramelize it with a hand-held propane torch. Lacking a torch, make a caramel sauce by combining 1 cup sugar with ½ cup water and 1 teaspoon lemon juice. Boil the mixture for 10 minutes or until it has caramelized, allow it to cool slightly, and then pour it over the tops of the *crème* while it is still warm. It will set to make a hard, brittle glaze.

Serves 8

219

Sweet Tamales *with*

Caramel Sauce

It may be stretching a point to call a filled cookie a tamale,
even if it does look like one. Nevertheless, the presentation is quite
appropriate to the locality and the cookie tastes pretty good, too.

¼ cup powdered sugar
1 egg yolk
¼ cup unsalted butter
1 teaspoon salt
1 tablespoon water
½ cup flour
8 ounces almond paste, softened
1 pint fresh strawberries, raspberries, or blueberries
8 sheets parchment paper, each measuring about 4½ inches square
Caramel Sauce (recipe follows)

Make the sauce first and set it aside to cool.

To make the *tamales,* combine the sugar, egg yolk, butter, salt, and water in a food processor and blend them. Add the flour and mix well. The mixture should be the consistency of cookie dough; it may be necessary to add a little more water.

Chop up the almond paste roughly and add the chunks to the dough in the food processor. Mix until all the ingredients are combined; again, the consistency should be that of a cookie dough.

Wash the fruit thoroughly; if you are using them, cut the strawberries in half, and set the fruit aside.

To assemble the *tamales,* divide the dough into 8 pieces and roll out each piece into a square measuring about 4 inches on each side. Place each square of dough onto a piece of parchment paper, which should be slightly larger than the dough. In the center of each square place about 1 tablespoon of the fresh fruit. Fold 2 sides of the dough over the filling and roll up the pastry and the parchment paper together, twisting the ends of the paper to secure the roll.

Steam the *tamales* for between 12 and 15 minutes; they are done when the pastry is no longer sticky or doughy and the parchment may be peeled off easily.

To serve, pour a pool of caramel sauce into the center of each plate, remove the parchment wrappings, and arrange 2 *tamales* per person on top of the sauce. The *tamales* should be hot; the sauce at room temperature.

Serves 4

CARAMEL SAUCE

1 cup sugar
½ cup water
1 teaspoon lemon juice
1 cup whipping cream

Mix the sugar, water, and lemon juice and bring the mixture to a boil. Reduce the heat until the mixture is boiling gently and continue to cook, stirring constantly, for between 8 and 10 minutes, or until the mixture is the color of caramel and has thickened. Gradually add the cream and bring the mixture back to a boil. Set the mixture aside to cool to room temperature; the sauce will thicken as it cools.

Makes about 1 ½ cups

Hiram Walker*

Raspberry Floating Islands♥

Oeufs à la neige is French for "snow eggs," a dessert that is essentially the same as the dish that Americans called "floating islands." It is extremely rich when prepared with the traditional crème anglaise made from egg yolks and milk. I have tried to lighten things up a good deal by using a fresh fruit sauce instead.

8 egg whites ⬧ 1 tablespoon lemon juice
1 cup sugar
¼ cup chopped walnuts or pistachio nuts (optional)
2 pints fresh raspberries; reserve 12 for garnish
Mint leaves, for garnish

Whip the egg whites until they form stiff peaks and gradually add 1½ teaspoons of the lemon juice and ½ cup of the sugar. Fold in the optional chopped nuts and then 1 pint of the raspberries. Using 2 large spoons, form the whites into mounds and poach them in gently simmering water for approximately 3 minutes on each side.

Purée the remaining pint of raspberries in a blender, add the remaining ½ cup sugar, and cook slowly until the sauce thickens. Add the remaining 1½ teaspoons lemon juice. Serve the sauce over the egg-white mounds and garnish them with fresh raspberries and mint.

Serves 4

*I developed this recipe for the *Food Arts*/Hiram Walker project. Hiram Walker liqueurs culinary flavors include 17 flavors that are great for cooking. Imported and marketed in the United States by Hiram Walker & Sons, Inc., Farmington Hills, MI.

Apple Tarts

Puff pastry is one of the high points of French cooking and, if taken one step at a time, not as formidable as it might seem. It does take time, from start to finish, but much of that time is spent, by the pastry dough, in resting in the refrigerator and, by the cook, in doing whatever else the cook wishes or needs to do. But see the footnote on page 120 for alternative sources of ready-made puff pastry if you prefer not to make your own.

Puff Pastry

1 pound (4 sticks) plus 6 tablespoons (¾ stick) butter, softened

3½ cups flour

1 cup water

1 teaspoon salt

Apple Filling

8 Granny Smith apples, peeled, cored, and sliced thin

1⅔ cups sugar

8 tablespoons (1 stick) butter, cut into very small cubes

Parchment paper

To make the pastry, sprinkle 1 pound of the butter lightly with some of the flour and mold it into a square measuring about 5 inches on each side. Combine the remaining 6 table-spoons softened butter with the rest of the flour, water, and salt in a food processor and process for 2 minutes. Roll out the dough, preferably on a marble slab to keep the pastry as cool as possible, into a rectangle measuring about 5 ½ inches by 10 inches and ½ inch thick. Set the slab of butter in the middle of the pastry and fold the two ends over the butter to enclose them. Wrap the dough in plastic wrap and refrigerate it for approximately 2 hours.

When it is thoroughly chilled, roll out the dough, and the butter inside it, lengthwise to make a rectangle measuring about 20 inches long and 8 inches wide. Fold the 8-inch sides over toward the center to make a 3-layer square of pastry. This is the first fold. Roll the square out again to a rectangle measuring 20 by 8 inches and, again, fold in the 8-inch sides. This is the second fold. Rewrap the pastry and refrigerate it for 2 hours.

When the pastry is again thoroughly chilled, roll it out twice more in the same manner for the third and fourth folds. Wrap and refrigerate for another 2 hours and again fold and roll twice more, for the fifth and sixth folds. Rewrap the pastry in plastic film and return it to the refrigerator until you are ready to make the tarts.

To make tarts, prepare the apple filling ingredients and set them to the side. Roll out the pastry until it is about ⅛ inch thick and cut out 40 circles each about 3 inches in diameter.

Preheat the oven to 375°F, line 2 large baking sheets with parchment paper, and arrange the pastry circles on the baking sheets. Cover each circle with a thin layer of apple slices, sprinkle on 1 cup of the sugar evenly over the layers, and dot with cubes of butter. Bake the pastries for approximately 15 minutes.

To assemble the servings, stack the pastries in layers of 4, flipping the top layer over so that it is pastry-side up. Sprinkle the remaining ⅔ cup sugar on top of the tarts and caramelize the sugar with a hand-held blow torch or by placing the tarts under a preheated broiler for approximately a minute, until the sugar is bubbly and beginning to caramelize.

Serves 10

RASPBERRY TART

This and the following lemon tarts always remind me of Paris, where even the tiniest pastry shop can be counted on for the most luscious, ripe fruits of the season. I always get a little homesick when I make them.

Sweet Dough
¼ cup powdered sugar
1 egg yolk
¼ cup unsalted butter
1 teaspoon salt ❧ 1 tablespoon water
½ cup flour
12-inch flan ring

Pastry Cream
2 cups milk
¾ cup sugar
4 egg yolks
¼ cup cornstarch

Topping
¾ cup raspberry or apricot preserves
2 pints fresh raspberries
Fresh mint leaves, for decoration

Raspberry Sauce
1 ½ pints fresh raspberries
⅓ cup sugar
Juice of 1 lemon

*T*o make the pastry, mix the sugar, egg yolk, butter, salt, and water in a food processor until blended. Add the flour and mix well (it may be necessary to add a little more water). The dough should be the consistency of cookie dough.

To make the pastry cream, boil the milk with ¼ cup of the sugar. Mix the egg yolks and the remaining ¼ cup sugar until creamy and add the cornstarch. Slowly whisk the egg-yolk mixture into the boiling milk and continue whisking the mixture until it boils again. Pour the pastry cream through a sieve into a bowl and let it cool over an ice bath.

To make a raspberry or apricot glaze, add about a tablespoon of water to the preserves to thin them and bring the mixture to a boil. Strain the glaze through a sieve into a clean pan and set aside.

For the sauce, purée the fresh raspberries, add the sugar and lemon juice, and cook the mixture over medium heat until it has thickened; this will take between 10 and 12 minutes. Stir frequently. Strain the sauce and set it aside.

Preheat the oven to 350°F. Roll out the dough until it is approximately ⅛ inch thick and line a 12-inch flan ring. Prick the dough with a fork. Bake the shell for between 10 and 12 minutes until golden brown. When the tart shell is cool, spread pastry cream into the shell and arrange the 2 pints of raspberries on top. Warm the glaze and brush it over the raspberries. To serve, pour 1 tablespoon of the raspberry sauce around each slice of tart and garnish with a mint leaf.

Serves 8

LEMON TARTS

*I adapted this recipe from a version made by my friend and mentor,
Jean Banchet, with whom I trained at the renowned restaurant,
Le Français, outside Chicago. The taste is really lemony.
In Arizona we are lucky because we have fresh, local lemons that are
intensely flavored because they are tree ripened. Even if you are not
so lucky, be sure to use fresh lemons and never lemon extract.*

Sweet Dough
1¼ cups powdered sugar
3 egg yolks
1 cup (2 sticks) plus 2 tablespoons butter
1 teaspoon salt
3 ounces water
3½ cups flour
8 3-inch tart molds

Lemon Filling
6 lemons
2¼ cups sugar
6 whole eggs
5 egg yolks
1¼ cups (2½ sticks) butter

To make the pastry, mix the sugar, egg yolks, butter, salt, and water together in a food processor for 4 or 5 minutes. Add the flour and mix for only a few seconds longer. Refrigerate the dough for 1 hour.

When the dough has been chilled, preheat the oven to 375°F. Roll out the dough until it is ⅛ inch thick and cut out 8 circles, each 4 inches in diameter. Line 8 individual, 3-inch tart molds, prick the pastry in the bottom with a fork, and bake for between 8 and 10 minutes, or until they are golden brown. Set the tart shells aside to cool before filling them.

To make the filling, grate the rind of 3 of the lemons and set it aside. Juice all 6 lemons. Place the rind, juice, sugar, whole eggs, and egg yolks into the top half of a double boiler set over simmering water and whisk the mixture until it is thick. This will take approximately 20 minutes; be sure not to allow the mixture to become hot enough so that the eggs scramble. Cut the butter into cubes and whisk them in increments into the egg mixture. Mix well.

Pour the filling into the cooled tart shells and chill them. Just before serving, glaze the tarts by placing them under a preheated broiler for approximately 1 minute, or until lightly browned on top. Serve at once.

Serves 8

Jalapeño & Orange Chutney Tarts

*In so many ways these tarts seem to sum up what my cooking has
evolved into over the past few years. The combination of ingredients
may seem odd and quite exotic, but it expresses the influence of several
food cultures that I have been fortunate enough to encounter.
While I was wondering what to do with a rather lackluster
orange tart I'd made, Leevon joked about my penchant
for putting* chile *peppers in everything. I thought, why not?
And that's how this wonderfully unorthodox tart came about.
Baked in a pastry shell, the chutney makes a light and refreshing
dessert. It may also be served as a relish for breads or on crackers,
with bagels at breakfast, or over cream cheese with crackers for an appetizer.*

Pastry
1 cup flour
1 teaspoon sugar
½ cup (1 stick) unsalted butter, cut into cubes
1 tablespoon water
10 3-inch tart molds

Chutney
10 oranges
1 tablespoon grated orange zest
2 tablespoons minced fresh roasted (page 266), peeled, and seeded *jalapeño* peppers
2 teaspoons peeled and minced fresh ginger
1 cup sugar ❧ 1 cup water
6 tablespoons honey

*T*o make the tart shells, combine the flour and sugar in a food
processor, add the butter and the water, and process only until a dough forms; overmixed dough is excessively elastic.
Wrap the dough in plastic and refrigerate it for 2 hours.

While the dough is chilling, make the chutney. Cut 4 of the oranges, unpeeled, into thin slices and set them aside. Grate the rind off one of the remaining oranges (there should be 1 tablespoon orange zest) and squeeze the juice out of all of them. Scrape the pulp out of the squeezed oranges and add it to the juice.

Combine the grated orange zest, juice and orange pulp, the *jalapeño* peppers, ginger, sugar, and water in a large sauce-pan. Cook the mixture slowly until the sugar is dissolved. Add the honey and the orange slices. Simmer for approximately 15 minutes or until the sliced oranges are transparent. Keeping the orange slices intact, drain the mixture through a strainer, reserving the liquid. Set the orange slices aside and reduce the liquid over low heat until it has thickened; this will take about 30 minutes. Combine the reduced liquid with the orange slices; you should have about 5 cups.

When the dough has chilled, preheat the oven to 350°F. Roll out the dough until it is ⅛ inch thick. Cut out 10 circles, each 4 inches in diameter, and fit them into 10 individual, 3-inch tart molds. Prick the pastry in the bottom of the molds and bake them for 15 minutes, or until they are golden.

To assemble the tarts, spoon the warm chutney into the warm tart shells and serve immediately.

Serves 10

PINE NUT, RAISIN, & CARAMEL TARTS

For years I had been making a walnut and raisin tart in caramel sauce that everyone thought was delicious. One day on a whim I thought it would be fun to use pine nuts—which are widely used in Southwest cookery. It worked and it's been a big success. Because of their high fat content, pine nuts will not keep as long as some other nuts will, so store them in an airtight container in the refrigerator or freeze them to extend their shelf life.

2 ½ cups sugar
Juice of half a lemon (2 tablespoons)
¼ cup water
1 ¼ cups heavy cream
½ cup (1 stick) butter
2 ½ cups pine nuts
1 ¼ cups walnuts
½ cup raisins (or more for a sweeter taste)
8 individual tart shells (page 228)

*P*repare the pastry for the tart shells, and while the dough is being chilled, make the caramel filling.

Combine the sugar, lemon juice, and water. Bring the mixture to the boil, turn the heat down to medium high, and stir constantly until the liquid has turned to an amber color; this will take approximately 15 minutes. Add the cream and butter carefully: The cream will splatter if added too quickly to the hot caramel. Continue stirring, over heat, until the ingredients are thoroughly mixed, about 1 minute. Set the saucepan in a bowl of ice water to stop the cooking. Add the pine nuts, walnuts, and raisins. Set the filling aside to cool to room temperature.

While the caramel is cooling, finish making the tart shells. Roll out the chilled dough, line 8 individual molds, and bake the pastry. Before filling the tarts, stir the mixture again to re-distribute the nuts and raisins and spoon the filling into the tart shells. As the mixture cools, it will become thick and more difficult to work with. If this occurs, warm slightly. Serve the tarts either at room temperature or chilled.

Serves 8

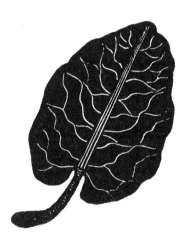

Banana, Chocolate, & Walnut Tarts

*My son, Daniel, who loves bananas and chocolate, was the inspiration
for this recipe, which we serve warm. These tartlets are wonderful
with fresh banana or vanilla ice cream and warm chocolate sauce.*

8 prebaked tart shells (page 228)
1 ½ ounces semisweet chocolate, chopped into small pieces
½ cup semisweet chocolate chips
1 cup whole walnut pieces
1 tablespoon plus 1 teaspoon rum
2 teaspoons vanilla extract
½ cup brown sugar ❧ 2 tablespoons butter
1 egg, slightly beaten ❧ 4 whole bananas

*B*ake the tart shells and set them aside to cool. Turn the oven
up to 400°F.

To make the filling, combine the chocolate pieces, chocolate chips, walnuts, rum, and vanilla in a mixing bowl and set
the mixture aside. Combine the brown sugar and butter in a
saucepan and heat until the butter is melted and the mixture is
very hot and gently boiling. Pour the butter mixture into the
bowl containing the chocolate, mix well, and add the beaten
egg, stirring it in thoroughly.

To assemble the tarts, slice half of a banana into each tart
shell and spoon chocolate mixture over the bananas; the mixture will form a mound in the shells. Bake the tarts for approximately 4 minutes, or until the top is slightly crunchy. Do
not overbake. Serve the tarts warm.

Serves 8

LEMON CRUST

*Here's an example of a culinary mistake that worked out just fine.
I was making a batch of lemon cookies but found that the
dough was too runny. Not wanting to waste the dough, I told my
pastry chef to put it on a baking sheet and cook it anyway.
The remarkable result was a cross between a cookie and a cake
and the taste was wonderful. We decided to call it lemon crust
and put it on the pastry cart. It was a big hit, especially when
served with a raspberry or orange sorbet.*

½ cup (1 stick) butter ✿ 1¼ cups sugar
1¼ cups flour ✿ 2 lemons
1 teaspoon baking powder
4 eggs

For the crust, preheat the oven to 350°F and butter and flour
an 8 by 8 by 1½-inch pan. Cream the butter with ¼ cup of the
sugar; add ¼ cup of the flour. Pat the dough into the jelly-roll
pan and bake the crust for between 10 and 15 minutes, or until it is golden brown.

While the dough is cooking, prepare the topping. Grate
the rind of 1 lemon. Juice both lemons, combine the juice and
the lemon rind, and set the mixture aside. Mix the remaining
1 cup of flour and the baking powder. Whisk the eggs, whisk
in the remaining 1 cup of sugar, the flour mixture, and the
lemon juice and rind. When the crust is ready, pour the topping over it and continue to bake the dessert for approximately 15 minutes longer. Serve cold.

Serves 8

Chocolate Macadamia Cakes *with* Warm Chocolate Grand Marnier Sauce

This dessert is incredibly rich and a few bites go a long way.
The combination of chocolate and macadamia nuts is wonderful and,
if you like Grand Marnier, you'll find that the intense essence and
natural affinity of the orange flavoring of the liqueur is perfect with both.
This is one of the quickest desserts you'll ever make.
The little cakes take only fifteen minutes to bake.

4 ounces semisweet chocolate
½ cup (1 stick) butter
3 eggs, separated
1 cup sugar
⅓ cup flour
½ cup whole macadamia nuts
Chocolate Grand Marnier Sauce (recipe follows)

To make the tarts, preheat the oven to 350°F and butter 4 individual 3-inch tart-shell molds.

Chop the chocolate into small pieces and melt them with the butter over low heat. Remove from heat to cool slightly so the eggs don't cook when you add them. Beat the egg yolks and add them to the chocolate mixture, blending well. In a separate bowl whip the egg whites with the sugar until they form stiff peaks. Fold the egg whites into the chocolate mixture and add the flour and nuts. Pour the batter into the buttered molds and bake the cakes for approximately 15 minutes.

While the cakes are baking, prepare the sauce. Serve the dessert at room temperature and the sauce warm.

Serves 4

CHOCOLATE GRAND MARNIER SAUCE

4 ounces semisweet chocolate
¼ cup whole milk
¼ cup Grand Marnier liqueur

Make the sauce while the cakes are baking. Chop the chocolate into small pieces and melt them over low heat with the milk. When the chocolate has melted, slowly add the liqueur. Keep the sauce warm until ready to serve.

WHITE & DARK CHOCOLATE

CHECKERBOARD MOUSSE

This dessert was inspired by a meal some of my customers had enjoyed at the famous Hotel Negresco in Nice, France. They came back with a sketch of the dessert on a cocktail napkin to show me. It was quite something: a checkerboard mousse cake with a layer of chocolate ganache between each square on the checkerboard. They challenged me to reproduce it and, after several attempts to figure out how it was done, I came up with the answer. It's really not that complicated. Bring it to the table, however, and your guests will be astounded by your dexterity at dessert making.

Dark Chocolate Mousse
8 ounces bittersweet chocolate
2 cups heavy cream

White Chocolate Mousse
1 envelope (¼ ounce) gelatin
¼ cup cold water
8 ounces white chocolate
2 cups heavy cream

Ganache
8 ounces bittersweet chocolate
1 cup heavy cream

*T*o prepare the dark chocolate mousse, break the chocolate into small pieces. Boil 1 cup of the cream, remove the pan from the heat, and add the chocolate. Stir until the chocolate is completely melted. Refrigerate the mixture. When it is cool, whip the remaining cup of cream and fold it into the chocolate mixture, mixing gently with a spatula until the cream is well blended. Pour into an 11 by 7 by 2-inch jelly-roll pan lined with parchment paper, cover with plastic wrap, and freeze for at least 4 hours. The mousse will be approximately ¾ inch to 1 inch deep.

To prepare the white chocolate mousse, stir the gelatin into the water and set the mixture aside for 5 minutes. When the gelatin has softened, prepare the mousse, following the directions above for dark chocolate mousse and stirring the softened gelatin into the mixture after the cream has been added. This mixture, too, needs to be frozen in a jelly-roll pan (as indicated above) for at least 4 hours.

To make the *ganache,* break the chocolate into small pieces. Boil the cream, remove the pan from the heat, and add the chocolate, stirring until the chocolate is completely melted. Cool the *ganache* in the refrigerator until it is silky, but still soft and easily spread. If it is used immediately, the heat will melt the mousse, so the *ganache* should be at room temperature or a little cooler. Half the *ganache* is used in the first step of assembling the desert; store the remainder in the refrigerator overnight, but remove it in time to return to room temperature before using it in the second step of the assembly.

The dessert is assembled in two separate steps. To begin with, cut each frozen mousse crosswise into 3 strips, each measuring approximately 3½ by 7 by 1 inch. Remove slices from the jelly-roll pan and spread *ganache* over the tops and around the sides of each strip of mousse. Using a platter that will fit into your freezer, stack the strips of mousse one on top of the other, starting with a strip of white mousse and alternating the colors. You will have a *ganache*-covered stack, or loaf, of 6 strips glued together by the *ganache* and about 6 inches high. Place the stack, unwrapped, into the freezer and leave it there overnight.

The following day cut the stack into 6 equal slices, as you would slice a loaf of bread. Each slice will consist of narrow strips of alternating white and dark chocolate mousse. Reassemble the loaf to create the checkerboard pattern: Place 1 slice of mousse flat on a platter with the strip of white mousse on the outside. On top, place a second slice turned so that there is a strip of dark mousse on the outside. Continue stacking the remaining slices in the same manner, alternating the colors of the outside strip. Frost the reassembled loaf with the remaining *ganache* and freeze again for 2 hours. When ready to serve, let cake thaw in refrigerator beforehand and serve cold.

Serves 12

Pumpkin Chocolate Brownies ♥

Despite its rich-sounding ingredients, this is actually a very sensible dessert that came from one of my chefs. It is reprinted here with permission from Better Homes & Gardens *magazine, which had asked us for a low-fat dessert for the holidays. These brownies will sate any sweet tooth without too many calories—unless you eat the whole pan.*

⅔ cup packed brown sugar ❧ ½ cup canned pumpkin
1 whole egg ❧ 2 egg whites
2 tablespoons vegetable oil ❧ 1 cup flour
1 teaspoon baking powder
1 teaspoon unsweetened cocoa powder
½ teaspoon ground cinnamon
½ teaspoon ground allspice ❧ ¼ teaspoon salt
¼ teaspoon ground nutmeg
⅓ cup miniature semisweet chocolate chips

Preheat the oven to 350°F and coat a 9 by 9 by 2-inch jelly-roll pan with nonstick cooking spray.

In a large mixing bowl, combine the brown sugar, pumpkin, egg, egg whites, and oil. Beat with an electric mixer on medium speed until the ingredients are blended. Add the flour, baking powder, cocoa powder, cinnamon, allspice, salt, and nutmeg. Beat on low speed until the batter is smooth. Stir in the chocolate chips.

Pour the batter into the prepared jelly-roll pan and spread it out evenly.

Bake for between 15 and 20 minutes, or until a toothpick inserted near the center comes out clean. Cool the cake in the pan on a wire rack. Cut into 2-inch squares.

Makes 15 brownies

Warm Chocolate Tortes

*I call this my "French brownie," and it's another of those great dishes
that originated by accident. One night I found that we were out of our
very popular flourless chocolate cake and had to bake some in a hurry.
It's not hard to make, but it takes some time to cool off.
Because we didn't have time, we just sent the miniature cakes to
the dining room straight out of the oven. The customers raved about
the dessert, so I refined the recipe somewhat and started baking
it in three-inch rings. The tortes are delicious with some fresh fruit
such as raspberries baked into them and fabulous with vanilla ice cream.
The flourless chocolate cake on which these tortes are based is a
straightforward recipe from Jean Banchet. See the variation
at the end of the recipe for the original version.*

1 pound semisweet chocolate
1 cup (2 sticks) unsalted butter
8 eggs, separated
1¾ cups sugar

Preheat the oven to 375°F. The tortes are baked in 3-inch
rings that have been buttered and floured and arranged on a
buttered and floured baking sheet.

Cut the chocolate into small pieces and melt them with the
butter in the top half of a double boiler set over boiling water,
or in a microwave oven on low power. Remove the pan from
the heat and set it aside briefly: It is important that the chocolate has cooled a bit so that the egg yolks do not cook when
they are added. Blend in the beaten egg yolks slowly to insure
all the ingredients are mixed well.

Whip the egg whites until they form stiff peaks, gradually adding sugar as you beat. When all the sugar has been added, fold in the chocolate mixture gently, blending well. Pour the batter into the rings and bake for approximately 10 minutes. Serve the tortes immediately.

Serves 8

VARIATION
Flourless Chocolate Cake
Use the same quantities and method but pour the batter into a greased and floured 8-inch cake pan and bake it at 375°F for approximately 45 minutes; a knife inserted into the center will come out clean when the cake is done. Set the cake pan on a rack and allow the cake to cool in the pan.

DARK CHOCOLATE TRUFFLES

*These are the bite-sized gourmandises that we present at the table
after dessert. That's the French way, and often such chocolates
are more extravagant and richer than the dessert itself.
I think it's a pleasant way of savoring the memory of a fine meal,
and they are nice to have around during the holidays when guests
drop over. They take to freezing extremely well.*

8 ounces dark chocolate, cut up into small pieces
4 tablespoons unsalted butter
½ cup heavy cream
2 tablespoons cocoa powder

Combine the chocolate, butter, and cream in the top half of a double boiler set over boiling water. Whisk until all the ingredients are melted together smoothly. Pour the mixture into a baking dish that measures 8 inches square and 2 inches deep. Refrigerate until the mixture hardens; this will take at least 4 hours.

Using a small melon baller, scoop the mixture out into balls. Roll the balls into cocoa powder and refrigerate them until they are to be served.

The mixture remaining in the pan can be melted down again and refrigerated and shaped in the same manner as the first batch.

Makes about 4 dozen truffles

VARIATION
Add 1 tablespoonful liqueur to the mixture when the chocolate is melted.

Sorbets & Ice Cream

Breathes there a soul who can withstand the temptation of freshly made sorbet or ice cream? We make all of our sorbets and ice cream fresh at Vincent's and people call us to order them for special parties or just to take home and indulge themselves. There really is a difference between store-bought and homemade.

So many of the newer cookbooks provide recipes for sorbets both innovative and classic and then finish off with half a sentence that runs: ". . . place the mixture in an ice cream maker and freeze according to manufacturer's directions." One might think that, without a machine, there is no sorbet, or ice cream for that matter. Not at all. The following recipes are all designed to be made in ice cream machines, but they can be made by hand, although the results will be more slushy than those made in machines.

To make sorbet and ice cream without using a machine, follow the directions for combining the ingredients to make the basic mixture and pour it into a shallow glass or stainless-steel container: An ice cube tray from which the partitions have been removed might be the handiest; a glass or stainless-steel baking dish will work just as well. Freeze the mixture until it is just beginning to freeze over but is still slushy. This may take anywhere from 30 minutes to an hour and a half, depending on the ingredients, the depth of the mixture in the container, and the temperature of your freezer. Well before it has solidified, turn the mixture into a bowl and whisk it until light and fluffy. Pour it back into the container and return to the freezer. When it has turned to slush for the second time— this may take only about 30 minutes because the mixture is already cold—whip it up again. For the best texture, repeat the entire procedure a third time; if you are pressed for time, continue with the recipe, omitting the third beating.

For sorbets, return the whipped-up slush to the freezer, cover, and freeze again for about 30 minutes before serving. If you have to keep the sorbet longer it will solidify. If this happens, about 30 minutes before serving, transfer it to the refrigerator to thaw out slightly. Ice creams may be served immediately or returned to the freezer, covered, and frozen again, for between 30 minutes and several hours.

SIMPLE SYRUP

1 cup sugar
1 cup water

Combine the sugar and water in a heavy saucepan and bring the mixture to a boil, making sure that all the sugar is dissolved. Set the pan aside until the mixture is cool. The syrup may be refrigerated and will keep for weeks.

Makes 1 1/4 to 1 1/2 cups

RASPBERRY SORBET ♥

4 baskets fresh raspberries or 3 packages (10 ounces each)
frozen and thawed raspberries in syrup
Juice of 1 lemon
1 to 1¼ cups sugar, the smaller quantity for frozen raspberries, the larger for fresh

*P*urée the raspberries in a food processor or blender and strain the purée through a fine sieve; you should have about 4 cups purée. Add the lemon juice and sugar, using the lesser quantity for a purée made of frozen raspberries.

Freeze in an ice cream maker, or sorbet machine, according to the manufacturer's instructions, or follow the directions on pages 245 to 246 for preparing without a machine.

Makes 1 to 1½ quarts

CHAMPAGNE SORBET

3 cups Simple Syrup (page 246)
1 bottle (750 ml; 3 cups) demi-sec Champagne
Juice of 2 medium lemons
1½ cups water

*C*ombine the cooled syrup with the Champagne, lemon juice, and water.

Freeze in an ice cream maker, or sorbet machine, according to the manufacturer's instructions, or follow the directions on pages 245 to 246 for preparing without a machine.

Makes approximately 2 quarts

PRICKLY PEAR SORBET♥

*When buying prickly pear fruit look for those that are firm to the touch,
but not hard. They should be a greenish-yellow to bright red but not
entirely green. The bright red ones will be the ripest, but be sure that
they are not too soft, which would indicate that they are overripe.*

*Fresh prickly pear fruit is available from late summer
through midwinter. When the fruit is sold in markets, the thorns will
most likely have been removed. If they have not, they can be removed
at home: Hold the fruit with a pair of metal tongs and scrub at the
prickles with a coarse brush until they are removed.*

*To obtain the juice from the fruit, peel off the skin and discard it. Cut off
the ends, cut the fruit in half lengthwise, and purée it to a fine pulp in a
food processor. Strain the purée through a fine sieve to remove any seeds.*

*The juice from the fruit can stain clothing so it's a good idea
to wear an apron and use metal utensils that won't get stained.
Processed prickly pear juice is available and may be used in place of
fresh juice. For the following recipe use two cups of juice. If you can't
find it in your local gourmet market, it can be ordered from Cahill
Desert Products in Phoenix, (602) 254-4815. It does, however, come
in 4¼-gallon pails, so, if that is not practical, one may use prickly pear
syrup, which comes from the same source, but in smaller quantities:
1-gallon and 12-ounce bottles. If you are using syrup,
use 1 cup of syrup and 1 cup of water. Omit the sugar entirely.*

20 prickly pear fruit (*tunas*), peeled and chopped roughly
Juice of half a lemon
⅓ cup sugar

$\mathcal{P}$urée the fruit in a food processor or blender and strain the juice. You should have about 2 cups. Add the lemon juice and sugar.

Freeze in an ice cream maker, or sorbet machine, according to the manufacturer's instructions, or follow the directions on pages 245 to 246 for preparing without a machine.

Makes approximately 2 cups

LEMON SORBET ♥

1 cup fresh lemon juice
1 cup mineral water
2 cups Simple Syrup (page 246)

Combine the lemon juice, mineral water, and syrup.

Freeze in an ice cream maker, or sorbet machine, according to the manufacturer's instructions, or follow the directions on pages 245 to 246 for preparing without a machine.

Makes approximately 1 quart

ORANGE SORBET ♥

4 cups fresh orange juice
1 cup sugar
Juice of 1 lemon

Blend the orange juice and sugar together and add the lemon juice.

Freeze in an ice cream maker, or sorbet machine, according to the manufacturer's instructions, or follow the directions on pages 245 to 246 for preparing without a machine.

Makes approximately 1 1/4 quarts

GRAPEFRUIT SORBET♥

4 cups fresh grapefruit juice
1 cup sugar

Combine the grapefruit juice and sugar.

Freeze in an ice cream maker, or sorbet machine, according to the manufacturer's instructions, or follow the directions on pages 245 to 246 for preparing without a machine.

Makes approximately 1 quart

PEACH SORBET♥

1 cup Simple Syrup (page 246)
6 peaches, peeled, pitted, and sliced
1 cup lemon juice

Bring the syrup to a boil. Add the sliced peaches and cook until the peaches become fluffy. Purée and strain the peach mixture and add the lemon juice.

Freeze in an ice cream maker, or sorbet machine, according to the manufacturer's instructions, or follow the directions on pages 245 to 246 for preparing without a machine.

Makes approximately 1 quart

VANILLA ICE CREAM

2 cups whole milk
2 cups half-and-half
2 whole vanilla beans, slit lengthwise but do not remove seeds
1 cup sugar
8 egg yolks

*H*eat the milk and half-and-half and bring the mixture to a boil. Add the vanilla beans and, stirring constantly, gradually add the sugar. Remove the pan from the heat. Add a little of the warm milk mixture to the egg yolks and whisk them thoroughly. When the milk mixture has cooled a bit, gradually add the egg yolk mixture, stirring constantly. Return the mixture to a very low heat and cook the custard, stirring it constantly for 8 to 10 minutes or until it is thickened. *It is important that the heat be very low so the egg yolks do not become scrambled.* As soon as the custard is thick enough to coat the back of the spoon, remove the pan from the heat and put it in an ice bath (a bowl containing ice cubes and water) to stop the cooking. Stir constantly so that the custard cools quickly. Pour the mixture through a strainer. (The vanilla beans can be used 2 or 3 times so don't discard them. Rinse them off, set them aside to dry, and store them in a jar of sugar.) Blend the custard in a blender until smooth. Freeze in an ice cream maker according to the manufacturer's instructions or follow the directions on pages 245 to 246 for preparing without a machine.

Makes 1 to 1 1/2 quarts

ARIZONA HONEY ICE CREAM

1 cup orange blossom honey
4 cups half-and-half
8 egg yolks

Mix the honey and half-and-half in a saucepan and bring the mixture to a boil. Remove the pan from the heat. Add a little of the warm liquid to the egg yolks and whisk them thoroughly. When the half-and-half mixture has cooled a bit, gradually whisk in the egg yolk mixture. Over very low heat and stirring constantly, cook the custard for between 4 and 5 minutes or until it is thickened. *It is important that the heat be very low so that the egg yolks do not become scrambled.* Remove the pan from the heat and put it in an ice bath (a bowl of ice cubes and water) to stop the cooking. Stir constantly to cool the mixture quickly. Freeze in an ice cream maker according to the manufacturer's instructions or follow the directions on pages 245 to 246 for preparing without a machine.

Makes 1 quart

CARAMEL ICE CREAM

1 ½ cups sugar • ⅓ cup water • 2 cups milk • 2 cups half-and-half • 8 egg yolks

Lightly grease a 9 by 13-inch baking sheet and set it aside.

Combine 1 cup of the sugar with the ⅓ cup water and bring the mixture to a boil. Reduce the heat to medium high and stir the mixture constantly until it is a caramel color; this will take approximately 10 to 12 minutes. Pour half of the caramel mixture onto the baking sheet and let it cool. (It will harden and be used at the end of the recipe.) To the remaining half of the caramel add the 2 cups of milk, bring the mixture to a boil, and then set the pan aside to cool.

In another saucepan combine the remaining ½ cup sugar and the half-and-half. Bring the mixture to a boil, then reduce the heat to low. Add a little of the hot cream mixture to the egg yolks and whisk them thoroughly. When the half-and-half mixture has cooled a bit, gradually add the egg yolk mixture to it. Stirring constantly and over very low heat, cook the custard for between 4 and 5 minutes or until it has thickened. *It is important that the heat be very low so the egg yolks do not become scrambled.* Remove the pan from the heat and put it in an ice bath (a bowl of ice cubes and water) to stop the cooking.

When the custard has cooled, add the caramel and milk mixture and freeze the mixture in an ice cream maker according to the manufacturer's instructions or follow the directions on pages 245 to 246 for preparing without a machine.

While the ice cream is freezing, break the hardened caramel into small pieces with a wooden spoon. When the ice cream is made, fold in the cracked caramel.

Makes 1 quart

WHITE CHOCOLATE ICE CREAM

10 ½ ounces white chocolate

4 cups milk

1 ⅓ cups sugar

8 egg yolks

Melt the chocolate in a double boiler until it is completely soft and smooth; this will take approximately 5 minutes. Let cool.

Heat the milk, add the sugar, and whisk in the beaten egg yolks. Cook the custard over medium-low heat for 2 or 3 minutes. Make sure that you stir the mixture constantly so that the egg yolks don't coagulate. Mix the chocolate with the custard and then chill the mixture well. Place the mixture in an ice cream machine for approximately 40 minutes or follow the directions on pages 245 to 246 for preparing without a machine.

Makes 1 ½ quarts

GOAT'S MILK ICE CREAM

*Goat's milk has a wonderful flavor, somewhat more
pronounced than that of cow's milk, with a little tanginess to it.
If you like goat's milk cheese, this should delight you.*

1 cup sugar
2 cups goat's milk
2 cups cow's milk
1 vanilla bean, slit lengthwise but do not remove seeds
8 egg yolks

Mix the sugar with the 2 kinds of milk and add the vanilla
bean. Bring the mixture to a boil and then reduce the heat.
Add a little of the hot milk to the egg yolks and whisk them
thoroughly. When the milk mixture has cooled a bit, gradually whisk in the egg yolk mixture and, stirring constantly,
over very low heat, cook the custard for between 4 and 5 minutes or until it has thickened. *It is important that the heat be very
low so that the egg yolks do not become scrambled.* Remove the
pan from the heat and put it in an ice water bath (a bowl of ice
cubes and water) to stop the cooking. Stir the custard constantly to cool it quickly. Pour the mixture through a strainer
(the vanilla bean can be used 2 or 3 times so don't discard it;
rinse it off, set it aside to dry, and store it in a jar of sugar) and
then blend it in a blender until it is smooth. Freeze the custard
in an ice cream maker according to the manufacturer's instructions or follow the directions on pages 245 to 246 for
preparing without a machine.

Makes approximately 1 quart

Drinks

The following section includes some of the more unusual drinks that we serve at Vincent's, mainly as aperitifs or cocktails. What to drink with the food is a matter of continuing fascination. French food and wine are so intimately entwined that the thought of one without the other is almost impossible even to contemplate. In general, Mexican food is much more casual and beer seems to be the best accompaniment. So, too, with my food: a full-bodied beer, perhaps an amber ale, will make a splendid partner.

When one combines the two culinary traditions as I do at Vincent's, the customs no longer apply. There are no real rules when it comes to pairing wines with Southwest cuisine. The intensity of the spices will vary, depending on how much is used, whether they are fresh or dried, and what varieties they are. It can be daunting to match a wine with a dish containing appreciable quantities of *chile* peppers.

Over the years my staff and I have developed some guidelines for pairing southwestern foods with wine. The really spicy dishes generally call for big, robust wines. The heavier meat and game dishes, those made with beef or venison, take best to Cabernet Sauvignons or Zinfandels from California or the Shiraz from Australia. Duck *confit,* too, can take a sturdy wine. Such wines need not be very complex, but the varietal nature of the grape should come through clearly. To stand up to the meat and the seasonings, the wines should have some tannin and enough acid to cut through the richness.

For dishes such as simply grilled meat and fowl, with slightly less hearty flavors, Pinot Noirs from California, Oregon, or France make good partners. Pinot Noir is also terrific with salmon, as are many other, lighter reds, such as Beaujolais, Valpolicella, and Rioja *tinto*. With other seafood, white wines always come to mind; they must have a crispness about them that refreshes the palate and a good deal of fruit to complement the lighter flavors of seafood. Sauvignon Blanc works well, as do Chardonnays from California, dry Rieslings from Alsace and Germany, and fine Sémillons from Bordeaux or California.

With appetizers I like sparkling wines and, being French, believe that Champagne goes with just about anything. The bubbles help cut the richness, and the coldness of the wine is refreshing at any time of the year.

Southwestern Iced Vodka

1 bottle (750 ml; 3 cups) vodka
Quarter of a *serrano chile,* including seeds
Quarter of a small hot yellow *chile,* including seeds
Quarter of a small, green *jalapeño chile,* including seeds
Quarter of a small, red *jalapeño chile,* including seeds

Combine the vodka and the *chiles* in the vodka bottle (you may have to pour some of the vodka out to make room for the *chiles*). Cover and let the mixture stand for 3 days at room temperature, then freeze. To serve, pour the vodka into chilled martini glasses. This will keep in the freezer for 6 months.

Makes one 750-ml bottle

Raspberry Vodka

1 bottle (750 ml; 3 cups) vodka
1 pint fresh raspberries

Pour out about a quarter of the vodka and set it aside. Add the raspberries to the bottle and top up with some of the reserved vodka. Let the mixture steep for 30 days. Do not strain out the raspberries; they stay in the bottle and are served with the vodka. Store in the freezer and serve icy cold.

Makes one 750-ml bottle

PRICKLY PEAR MARGARITAS

¾ cup tequila
½ cup Triple Sec liqueur
1 cup fresh lime juice
1 tablespoon sugar
2 tablespoons prickly pear syrup (see glossary)

Combine the tequila, Triple Sec, lime juice, sugar, and prickly pear syrup in a blender. Fill 4 margarita glasses with ice and divide the mixture among them.

Serves 4

ORANGE-BLOSSOM HONEY COOLERS

¼ cup orange-blossom honey
¼ cup lemon juice
¼ cup orange juice
1 cup white rum
1 teaspoon grated nutmeg
2 slices orange and 2 slices lemon, halved, for garnish

Combine the honey, lemon juice, orange juice, rum, and nutmeg with ice and shake well until the honey is blended in. Serve ¼ cup of the mixture poured over 1 cup ice to each person as an aperitif. Garnish each glass with half slices of orange and lemon.

Serves 4

APRICOT CHAMPAGNE

1 teaspoon apricot liqueur
1 teaspoon apricot brandy
Champagne or sparkling wine

*F*or each serving, pour the apricot liqueur and the apricot brandy into a Champagne flute. Pour iced Champagne on the top and serve immediately.

Serves 1

WHITE WINE SANGRIA

2 fresh peaches, peeled and sliced
1 cup fresh strawberries, washed and hulled
½ cup fresh raspberries, cleaned
2 tablespoons sugar
1 bottle (750 ml; 3 cups) chilled fruity white wine

*P*lace the fruit into a large pitcher, sprinkle it with sugar, and let the fruit macerate for between 2 and 4 hours in the refrigerator. Shortly before serving, add the wine; I would recommend a chablis.

Serves 4 to 6

Red Fruit & Champagne

½ cup fresh strawberries, washed and hulled ❧ ½ cup fresh raspberries, cleaned
¼ cup red currants, cleaned ❧ ¾ cup sugar
1 bottle (750 ml; 3 cups) chilled Champagne or sparkling wine
¼ cup raspberry liqueur

*P*lace the fruit in a large pitcher and cover with the sugar in a layer. Allow the fruit to macerate in the refrigerator for between 2 and 3 hours. Just before serving, pour a bottle of Champagne over the fruit and add the raspberry liqueur. Serve chilled.

Serves 4 to 6

Citrus Wine

3 blood oranges ❧ 1 pink grapefruit
1 vanilla bean ❧ 1 stick cinnamon
1 teaspoon tequila ❧ 1 bottle (750 ml; 3 cups) rosé wine
1 cup sugar

*W*ash but do not peel the oranges and grapefruit and cut them into quarters. In a large bowl, combine the citrus fruit, vanilla bean, cinnamon, tequila, and wine. Cover and let the mixture steep, unrefrigerated, for 20 days. The mixture should be kept in a cool, dark place such as a pantry or cellar. After 20 days, add 1 cup sugar and let the mixture stand for another 10 days. Strain the mixture, bottle it, and serve the wine at room temperature.

Serves 4 to 6

Miscellaneous Basic Preparations

This section of the book is a catch-all for recipes that are not dishes in themselves but the building blocks for many of my recipes. Here you'll find directions for grilling whole heads of garlic, for roasting and peeling *chile* peppers, for making various stocks, and for making that most useful of sauces, the traditional French *beurre blanc* and a number of variations, some absolutely Southwestern.

When my recipes call for stock, I think it's almost always better if you can use homemade stock rather than canned. Stocks can be made in big batches and frozen so that, when you need to have some, you can just take it out and use it. If you really think you won't have the time, patience, or energy to make stock yourself, call your favorite restaurant and buy it by the pint or quart as you need it. They should be able to accommodate you and you'll appreciate the difference later. In a pinch, canned will work but the real stuff really is better.

FISH STOCK

5 pounds fish bones and heads, cut in medium-sized pieces*
1 leek, green part only
2 whole onions, peeled and quartered
1 cup parsley stems
1 stalk celery, including leaves

Put the fish, leek greens, onions, parsley, and celery into a large stock pot and cover with approximately 8 quarts water. Bring the mixture to a boil, then turn down the heat and simmer for approximately 30 minutes. Strain and reduce until you have approximately 4 quarts. Freeze.

Makes 4 quarts

*Ask your favorite restaurant to save them for you or obtain them from the fish market.

CHICKEN STOCK

5 pounds chicken or turkey bones*
2 whole onions, peeled and quartered
1 stalk celery, including leaves
1 leek, green part only
1 head garlic
½ cup parsley stems
1 sprig fresh rosemary or 1 teaspoon dried rosemary
1 sprig fresh thyme or 1 teaspoon dried thyme
1 tablespoon kosher salt
1 teaspoon whole black peppercorns

Put the bones, onions, celery, leek greens, garlic, parsley, rosemary, thyme, salt, and peppercorns into a large stock pot and cover with approximately 8 quarts water. Bring the mixture to a boil, then reduce the heat and simmer for approximately 1½ hours. Strain the stock and freeze it until you are ready to use it.

Makes 6 quarts

*When cooking with chicken or turkey, save the bones for stock by tossing them into a plastic bag and freezing them until you have enough for a stock. Or you can ask your butcher to save them for you. Turkey bones will yield the same taste as chicken bones.

CHICKEN GLAZE

Chicken glaze is stock that has been strained and reduced to a dark, thick syrup. Omit the salt if you are making a glaze. Reduce the stock very slowly by simmering it in a thick pan to avoid burning or scorching. A quart of stock will take approximately 1 1/2 hours to reduce to 1 tablespoon. Glaze can be kept refrigerated for weeks or stored in the freezer for months. It is used to enhance the flavor of certain foods or as a glossy coating for both hot and cold dishes.

DUCK STOCK

3 whole duck carcasses*
3 tablespoons tomato paste
1 head garlic
1 carrot, peeled and coarsely chopped
1 onion, peeled and quartered
2 whole tomatoes, quartered
1 tablespoon whole black peppercorns
1 teaspoon kosher salt
1 whole bay leaf
1 sprig fresh rosemary or 1 teaspoon dried rosemary
1 sprig fresh thyme or 1 teaspoon dried thyme
6 quarts veal stock or water

Preheat the oven to 400°F. Roast the duck carcasses for approximately 20 minutes or until they are lightly browned. Put them into a stock pot and add the tomato paste, garlic, carrot, onion, tomatoes, peppercorns, salt, bay leaf, rosemary, and thyme. Cover with 6 quarts veal stock or water. (The veal stock will make a richer tasting duck stock but if none is available, water is fine.) Bring the mixture to a boil and simmer for approximately 3 hours. Strain and cool.

Makes approximately 3 quarts

*Obtain the duck carcasses from your favorite restaurant or butcher.

Veal Stock

5 pounds veal bones*
1 cup tomato paste
5 medium tomatoes, quartered
4 medium onions, peeled and quartered
2 stalks celery, chopped
1 leek, green part only
1 head garlic, cut in half horizontally
2 whole bay leaves
½ cup parsley stems
1 sprig fresh rosemary or 1 teaspoon dried rosemary
1 sprig fresh thyme or 1 teaspoon dried thyme
2 tablespoons whole black peppercorns
1 tablespoon kosher salt

Preheat the oven to 400°F. Roast the veal bones in a shallow baking dish for approximately 30 minutes or until they are browned.

Remove them from the pan and place all bones in a large stock pot. Add the tomato paste and cover the bones with 8 quarts of water. Add the tomatoes, onions, celery, leek greens, garlic, bay leaves, parsley, rosemary, thyme, peppercorns, and salt. Bring the mixture to a boil, turn the heat down, and simmer for approximately 6 hours. Strain the mixture and cool the stock in an ice-water bath.

Makes approximately 4 quarts

Roasted Chile Peppers

Roast chile peppers over a hot grill, a gas flame, or under the broiler, turning them frequently until the skin is blackened and blistered all over. Place the peppers in a plastic or a brown-paper bag and close the top, or in a bowl covered with a plate, and set them aside to cool. The container must be closed to keep in the steam. When the peppers are cool enough to handle, peel off the thin skin and discard it. Some people do this under water to keep from irritating the skin and eyes; others declare that the water washes away the taste. Remove the inner ribs and seeds, which are the hottest parts of the chile, and the peppers are ready to be used in a recipe.

*When you cook with veal or other meats save the bones for stock. Just toss them in a plastic bag that you keep in the freezer until you have enough to make a good stock. Some butchers will save bones for their customers.

BEEF & CHICKEN STOCK

5 pounds beef bones
10 pounds chicken bones and backs
1 onion, peeled and halved
5 carrots, peeled
1 stalk celery
2 bay leaves

In a large stock pot, combine the beef and chicken bones, add the onion, carrots, celery, and bay leaves, and pour in 8 quarts water. Bring the mixture to a boil, reduce the heat, and simmer for approximately 1½ hours.

Strain the stock, discarding the solids. Return the liquid to the cleaned pan and reduce over medium heat to 1 quart; this will take approximately another 1 to 1½ hours.

This stock is very gelatinous and will solidify when cool. It may be refrigerated for 2 or 3 days, or kept frozen.

Makes 1 quart

GRILLED OR ROASTED GARLIC ♥

*When we tell people that the grilled garlic is edible and not just for
presentation, they often express the belief that it must be too strong
and no one will come near them for a week. Actually just the opposite
is true. Once the garlic is grilled, it becomes as soft as butter,
and the taste becomes very mild. Use it on bread or just eat it as is.
Garlic is also considered to be beneficial for your heart.*

2 whole heads garlic, top and root ends cut off

Place the garlic heads over a medium-hot grill and cook them, turning frequently. They should be browned, not blackened. If a grill is not available, they may be roasted for 45 minutes at 325°F.

When cooked, the garlic cloves will be very soft and can be spread like butter. The taste is mild and quite delicious.

Makes 2 tablespoons

BEURRE BLANC

A superb sauce in the original, beurre blanc *also takes very
kindly to additional flavorings. With very little trouble one has
a repertoire of interesting sauces at one's fingertips. The flavorings
are added at the last minute, after the cream and butter
have been whisked into the basic sauce.*

1 cup white wine
1 cup white wine vinegar
1 tablespoon chopped shallots
1 tablespoon heavy cream
1 pound (4 sticks) unsalted butter, cut into 8 cubes

Put the wine, vinegar, and shallots in a skillet and reduce the mixture over moderate heat until the liquid is completely gone and only
the shallots remain. Whisk in the cream and softened butter, 1 cube
at a time. Serve the sauce hot, but do not allow it to boil.

Makes 2 cups; serves 8

VARIATIONS

Ancho Chile *Beurre Blanc*
1 tablespoon pure ancho chile powder
Serve with venison and wild boar.

Basil *Beurre Blanc*
¼ cup chopped basil
Serve with seafood.

Chipotle *Beurre Blanc*
1 tablespoon puréed *chiles chipotle en
adobo* (canned, pickled *chipotle chiles*
in adobo sauce)
Serve with veal and mild-flavored game,
such as quail and rabbit.

Chive *Beurre Blanc*
¼ cup chopped chives
Serve with mild fish, such as halibut and
sea bass.

Cilantro *Beurre Blanc*
¼ cup chopped cilantro
Serve with seafood and *tamales.*

Dill *Beurre Blanc*
¼ cup chopped dill
Serve with salmon.

Italian Parsley *Beurre Blanc*
¼ cup chopped flat-leaf, Italian parsley
Serve with mild fish, such as halibut and
sea bass.

Jalapeño *Beurre Blanc*
¼ cup *jalapeño* pepper, roasted, peeled,
seeded, and diced (page 266)
Serve with lobster or shrimp.

Lime *Beurre Blanc*
Juice and zest of 2 limes
Serve with chicken.

Tarragon *Beurre Blanc*
¼ cup chopped tarragon
Serve with chicken.

Tomato *Beurre Blanc*
¼ cup peeled, seeded, and diced tomato
1 tablespoon tomato paste
Stir in ½ cup chopped fresh basil and
serve with basil pasta.

Whole-Grain Mustard *Beurre Blanc*
¼ cup whole-grain mustard
Serve with veal.

Glossary

NOTE: Words that appear in SMALL CAPS are themselves defined in this glossary.

ACIDULATED WATER. Water to which a little bit of vinegar or lemon juice has been added.

ADOBO SAUCE. A mild vinegar and onion sauce in which CHILES CHIPOTLES are canned and sold as *chiles chipotles en adobo.*

'AHI TUNA. Bigeye or yellowfin tuna; culinarily, the most favored of the species.

ANASAZI BEANS. Named after the Anasazi (Navaho for Ancient Ones), a Native American people who flourished in the Southwest after 100 A.D. and who began cultivating beans after 500 A.D.; the beans are fairly large and interestingly mottled red and white.

BLACK BEANS. Also called turtle beans, these have been known to Mexican cooks for at least seven thousand years. In Mexico they are customarily used in soups; in the Southwest they are as often used in salads and CHÍLIS.

BLACK-EYED PEAS. Also called cowpeas and actually a bean; their colloquial name is derived from the black rim to be seen on the inner curve of the coat seam. Of Asian origin, these beans were brought to America by African slaves. Combined with red and green peppers, green onions, and vinegar, they make a dish called "Texas caviar."

BLUE CORN. Originally grown by the Pueblos, a blue-gray variety of corn that is usually dried and made into cornmeal.

CHILE PEPPERS. One of the glories of southwestern cookery, the *chile* pepper is the fruit of a plant used extensively in the New World and divided into five species. Most of the common culinary *chiles* belong to the species *Capsicum annuum* and are used—fresh and dried—in every conceivable way: roasted, cooked in soups and stews, stuffed, pickled, eaten raw, and now even in desserts.

Most *chile* peppers are hot, but the pungency varies even among individual *chiles* of the same kind. In 1912 a pharmacologist, Wilbur Scoville, developed a measure, in what he called Scoville Units, that ranged from 0 to 300,000. It was based on the reaction of human tasters to solutions of *chile* peppers in alcohol and sugar water. That measure, though still widely quoted, has been replaced by high-pressure liquid chromatography, which may be handy for the botanists but is less useful for the cook in the marketplace. In the descriptions below, a rough and ready gauge of hotness on a scale of 1 to 10 has been used with the caveat that it is approximate. Sweet banana peppers and bell peppers would register 0; JALAPEÑOS would register 5, the halfway mark.

For many years botanists themselves had trouble coming to any agreement about the scientific classification of the fruit; even today, common names are subject to creative variations: the same name may be used for more than one variety or the same *chile* may be known under numerous aliases. The common names of the varieties called for in this book are listed below.

ANAHEIM. *See* NEW MEXICO

ANCHO. The POBLANO when dried; dark reddish-brown and mildly hot (3 on a scale of 10); varieties may be called *mulato* (light brown) or *negro* (black).

CALIFORNIA. *See* NEW MEXICO

CASCABEL. A cultivated variety of the *chile mirasol*; a round, shiny, dark red pepper, the size of a large cherry; usually sold dried. The skin is almost translucent and the seeds inside rattle. *Cascabels* are fairly hot: 5 on a scale of 10.

CHIMAYÓ CHILE. *See* NEW MEXICO

CHIPOTLE. The ripe JALAPEÑO when smoked and dried. It is hot: 5 on a scale of 10. Available simply dried (in which case they are usually rehydrated by being soaked in water for about 30 minutes) or canned in a mild pickle sauce and sold as *chiles chipotles en adobo*.

GÜERO. The Spanish word for blond, this is a generic name for any hot, yellow *chile,* but usually refers to yellow wax peppers. Depending on the variety, the pungency ranges from mild to very hot: many are between 5 and 8 on a scale of 10; some are only 3.

HABANERO. An extremely hot (10 on a scale of 10), small, round, yellow-orange *chile* pepper that in Jamaica is known as Scotch, or Scots, bonnet and in the Bahamas as the Bahamian or Bahamian Mama. It is usually used in sauces and barbecue recipes and is said, by those who have acquired a taste for it, to have overtones of apricot.

JALAPEÑO. A smooth, dark green or, when ripe, bright red *chile* that is stubby, about two inches long, and hot (5 on a scale of 10), the *jalapeño* is the most widely consumed *chile* in the United States. Dried and smoked *jalapeños* are called CHIPOTLES.

NEW MEXICO. A large, almost rectangular *chile,* measuring about six or seven inches in length; available fresh in both its red and green forms and, when ripened, dried and roasted. At between 2 and 4 on a scale of 10, it is not extremely hot. It is also called the California *chile* and was formerly called the Anaheim, a name that is still used in California where, because the growing conditions are different, the *chiles* are milder. Chimayó *chiles* are a subgroup long grown in the Chimayó valley of New Mexico; they are hotter (6 on a scale of 10) and have thinner skins. When dried, the red ones are sometimes called *chiles colorados,* the green ones *chiles posados.*

PASILLA. A wrinkled, dark brown, dried *chile* (fresh, it is the *chile chilaca*) that is mildly hot (3 on a scale of 10). The Spanish name means "little raisin," a reference to the color.

POBLANO. A wide-shouldered, almost heart-shaped, very dark green pepper that turns a dark red when ripe. Usually mild (3 on a scale of 10), the pungency of these *chiles* seems to be particularly variable. The fresh ANCHO are usually served stuffed, as *chiles rellenos.* They are frequently sold (and even referred to in recipes) as *pasilla chiles,* an odd misnomer as they are neither dried nor particularly raisinlike.

SERRANO. Widely available, the *serrano* (meaning "from the mountains") is a small, slim, very hot *chile* (6 or 7 on a scale of 10), usually sold green but also available red. Indigenous to the mountains of northern Puebla and Hidalgo in Mexico, these *chiles* are now widely available, are most commonly used in fresh salsas, and are extremely good when pickled *en escabeche.*

CHILES RELLENOS. Stuffed *chiles.*

CHILI. The dish, as distinguished from the pepper, that is to be found all over the Southwest and West: a stew of beans and meat flavored with CHILI POWDER or *chile* peppers. It should be noted that, for some aficionados, beans are anathema.

CHILI POWDER. A blended spice mixture, first made commercially in 1894 by William Gebhardt, who owned a café in New Braunfels, Texas. Used to flavor CHILI. It consists of dried, ground *chiles* mixed with cumin, oregano, garlic, cayenne and black pepper, and salt. It is no substitute for the *chile* pod itself; in this book we distinguish between chili powder (the commercial mix) and *chile* powder (the pure, ground pod of a particular variety).

CILANTRO. The Spanish word for fresh coriander; also called Chinese parsley.

FRIJOLES. Mexican for beans of any kind, although the word is usually applied to PINTO BEANS.

JÍCAMA. A mild, white-fleshed root vegetable with a crunchy texture; often used in salads and as a refreshing counterpoint to hot *chiles.*

MASA HARINA. Cornmeal prepared especially for *tortillas.* The corn is dried, treated with slaked lime, and boiled until it is soft, and then dried again before being ground into flour.

NOPALES. The "leaves" of the prickly pear cactus, also known as cactus paddles; these may be eaten raw or cooked and served as a vegetable or as a filling for *tacos.* See page 187 for directions for removing the spines. The fruit, the eponymous prickly pear, is called TUNA in Spanish.

PIÑONES. Pine nuts; called *pignoli* in Italy. Gathered in the Southwest from small pine trees, they are very expensive. They may be eaten raw, but are better toasted, which must be done carefully, because they burn in a twinkling.

PINTO BEANS. A large, mild-flavored (some call it dull) variety of the kidney bean, streaked beige and pink. When cooked it turns a pinkish gray.

QUELITAS. Better known as lamb's lettuce or *mâche,* these greens may be cooked as a vegetable, but are more often served in salads; the flavor and texture is similar to that of spinach.

TUNA. Prickly pear; the fruit of the prickly pear cactus. It has a sweet aroma, like that of a melon. The juice may be used fresh or preserved as a syrup.

ZEST. The outer layer of a citrus fruit. Only the colored portion of the fruit is considered the zest.

Index

274

Index